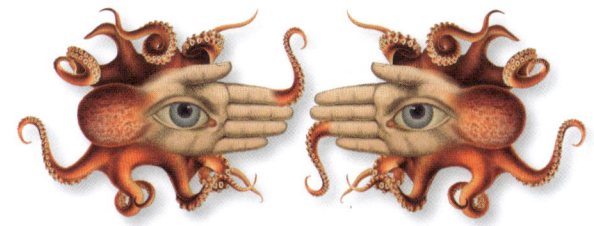

BOADICEA'S TAROT
of Earthly Delights

CAROLINE KENNER, Author
with PAULA MILLET, Deck Creator *and* Artist

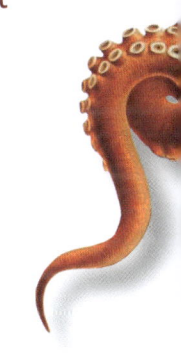

REDFeather™
MIND | BODY | SPIRIT

4880 Lower Valley Road, Atglen, PA 19310

Copyright © 2025, text by Caroline Kenner, illustrations by Paula Millet
Originally published in 2024 © Boadicea Design, LLC, text by Caroline Kenner, deck by Paula Millet

Library of Congress Control Number: 2024951332

All rights reserved. No part of this work may be reproduced or used in any form or by any means—graphic, electronic, or mechanical, including photocopying or information storage and retrieval systems—without written permission from the publisher.

The scanning, uploading, and distribution of this book or any part thereof via the Internet or any other means without the permission of the publisher is illegal and punishable by law. Please purchase only authorized editions and do not participate in or encourage the electronic piracy of copyrighted materials.

"Red Feather Mind Body Spirit" logo is a trademark of Schiffer Publishing, Ltd.
"Red Feather Mind Body Spirit Feather" logo is a registered trademark of Schiffer Publishing, Ltd.

Deck, collage illustrations, and graphic design by Paula Millet
Book by Caroline Kenner with Paula Millet
Type set in Baskerville/Calibri/Dalliance OT/Bodoni Ornaments

Custom Tarot spreads by Sara Mastros, courtesy of Fool's Dog, LLC
Edited by Kayt Lewis and Anna M.J. Holloway

ISBN: 978-0-7643-6908-7
Printed in China

Published by REDFeather Mind, Body, Spirit
An imprint of Schiffer Publishing, Ltd.
4880 Lower Valley Road
Atglen, PA 19310
Phone: (610) 593-1777; Fax: (610) 593-2002
Email: Info@redfeathermbs.com
Web: www.redfeathermbs.com

For our complete selection of fine books on this and related subjects, please visit our website at www.redfeathermbs.com. You may also write for a free catalog.

REDFeather Mind, Body, Spirit's titles are available at special discounts for bulk purchases for sales promotions or premiums. Special editions, including personalized covers, corporate imprints, and excerpts, can be created in large quantities for special needs. For more information, contact the publisher.

We are always looking for people to write books on new and related subjects. If you have an idea for a book, please contact us at proposals@schifferbooks.com.

ACKNOWLEDGMENTS

Creating *Boadicea's Tarot of Earthly Delights* has been a wonderful experience. I am very grateful that I had both the time and the inspiration to produce a fully illustrated Tarot deck. It had been a dream of mine for many years.

I am thankful to the many individuals who supported me along the way:

- My husband, Dale; our daughter, Lydia; and my sister, Andrea, for their
  unflagging interested and positive feedback throughout the long illustration process. They greeted each new card with heartwarming praise.

- Dear friends and fellow Tarot aficionados: Cheryl Fair, Kayt Lewis, and Deborah Shuman for encouraging me to manifest my Tarot card visions into a tangible deck. As well as to the extensive online community of Tarot deck creators, many of whom have both encouraged and advised me so generously.

- My museum colleagues, who were often amused by my curious juxtapositions of classic art, natural-history illustrations, and miscellaneous oddities.

- And, of course, to Caroline Kenner and Jason Linhart for adding the deck to their fabulous compendium of Tarot apps. From the very onset I envisioned *Boadicea's Tarot* as a Fool's Dog app and was thrilled when they chose to include my work with all those wonderful decks.

Beyond my gratitude to Fool's Dog, I am especially grateful to Caroline for her decision to collaborate with me in this endeavor. Her authorship of the companion book has brought a level of wisdom, whimsy, and gravitas to the project that I could not have even dreamed of.

–Paula Millet

ACKNOWLEDGMENTS

I am grateful to my husband, Jason Linhart, and our daughter, Sophie. Jason and I have really enjoyed working together on our company, The Fool's Dog. Jason helped me transform a lifelong avocation into a vocation.

In Witchcraft, I am grateful to the many friends who have walked the Witches' Path alongside me over the course of four decades. Love, gratitude, respect to Connie, Ann & John, Stef, Gloria & David, MAC, Celene & Colleen, Diotima & Rebecca, Judika, Cat & Richard, H. Byron, Katrina Messenger, Hecate Demeter, Gwendolyn, Pamela, Alison C., Sara M., Amy B., April & Jim, Chris F., Sabrina, Catalina, Nell, Caine, Rebecca Rose, Rose & DK, Debby & Zan, Emily I., Irene & Ash, and, posthumously, Brianna; also, the graduates of Gryphons Grove, the folx of Sacred Space, our dear Soiree family, and my beloved friends in the Assembly of the Sacred Wheel, the Universal Temple of Spirits, Reflections Mystery School, Blue Star Witchcraft, the Asheville Mother Grove Goddess Temple, the CUUPS folx at the Unitarian Universalist Congregation of Frederick, and in Heathenry, Urglaawe, and ADF Druidry.

I am grateful for dear friends among Sandra Ingerman's senior students, especially Melissa, Renna, Michele Grace, Mary Beth, Karen F., Stuart & Anne, Toni & Mara, and, posthumously, Alice, Thelma, and Carol.

Love, respect, and gratitude to my Tarot sisters, Ellen, Joanna, Christine, Alexandra, Thalassa, and Cat Dubh, and to Tarot's beloved lodestars, Rachel Pollack and Mary K Greer.

I am extremely grateful to my alma mater, Bryn Mawr College, and to my lifelong friends from college. Anassa Kata!

I am very grateful to collaborate with Paula Millet. I consider Paula to be a genius-level graphic artist.

Finally, I give thanks for The Fool's Dogs: Lola Montez, Dexter Gordon, Oscar Peterson, Edgrr Allan Poe, and the current title holder: Rupert Brooke.

—Caroline Kenner

···· CONTENTS ····

Creators' Statements 6
Overview
    Tarot Beginnings. 9
    Boadicea the Queen 13
    Why The Garden of Earthly Delights? 15
The Major Arcana 16
The Minor Arcana 65
    Suit of Combustion 70
    Suit of Tentacles. 98
    Suit of Æther. 126
    Suit of Fungi 154
    The Perspicacious Platypus. 182
Divination. 184
Reading Tarot. 187
Tarot Spreads
    One, Two, Three, and Five Cards 190
    Boadicea's Badassery. 192
    The Spirit Spread 193
    Time after Time 194
    Modern Celtic Cross 194
    Grand Garden of Earthly Delights 196
    Boadicea's Chariot 198
    The Hamsa of Protection. 200
    Boadicea's Saga Spread. 202
Finally: Take Off the Training Wheels and Go! 204
Appendix: Image Sources and Credits. 206
About the Authors. 216

CREATORS' STATEMENTS

Paula Millet: Deck Creator, Designer, Principal of Boadicea Design, LLC

I appreciate Tarot primarily for its visual presentation of rich and complex symbolism, and because there is a story in every card.

I first encountered the Tarot during college, when a dear friend introduced us. The visual storytelling and the symbolism captivated me instantly. This fascination endured. Over the years, I bought some decks and guidebooks, and began reading Tarot for myself.

In 2013, I began noodling around with Photoshop collage and Tarot, designing versions of a few Tarot cards, just for fun. Initially I wasn't focused on producing an entire deck, just enjoying the process. But very soon I realized I was creating a fully illustrated Tarot. The spirit of the deck compelled me, and I spent almost five years studying Tarot iconography and composing the card art.

In addition to classic Rider-Waite-Smith imagery, the inspiration for the illustrations comes from my lifelong love of classic art, natural sciences, and all manner of museums. Growing up, our family went to a museum, botanical garden, zoo, historic house, etc., nearly every week. These experiences enriched my visual vocabulary and set the stage for my career as a museum exhibition designer. I recently retired from the Smithsonian and now work as a freelance exhibition and graphic designer.

In the 2000s I was the chief of design at the Walters Art Museum in Baltimore, Maryland, where I was both beguiled and bemused by their collection of Renaissance through early-nineteenth-century paintings. I found these artworks to be ideal source material for my Tarot art. The lush realism and dramatic storytelling of the paintings inspired the aesthetic style of *Boadicea's Tarot*.

To find component images for the cards, I scrolled though innumerable public-domain online image collections. I pored over portraits, searching for images that exquisitely captured the personalities of the sitters, seeking just the right face, posture, or outfit. Then I dissected and recombined these elements to create a Tarot character. Portraits are particularly compelling as illustrations for Tarot cards because the subject's direct gaze, per the original artist's intent, breaks the "fourth wall" and speaks directly to the viewer.

In addition to the characters for my cards, I also searched for landscapes, interiors, and creatures both weird and mundane. Sometimes I held an image in my mind as I searched. But often, my discoveries were purely serendipitous. I would stumble upon the perfect face, or the perfect fish, and add it to my source files. In many cases, such as in my Hermit or the Two of Wands, I felt that the images themselves told me which card they were supposed to become.

Technically, I work in Adobe Photoshop, sampling, manipulating, and blending select bits from at least five or six or up to more than a dozen images to create each digital illustration. Many of the sampled artworks are not particularly well known, since the source works were not always material to the card meanings. But I have also included a few recognizable components from famous works, scattered like Easter eggs for sharp-eyed art history fans.

Boadicea's Tarot is much more to me than the sum of its parts. The whole creation is imbued with the fierce spirit of the warrior queen Boadicea. I am inspired by the often-inexplicable whimsy of a realm beyond our everyday reality. The project has allowed me to share my vision, intuition, and even my sense of humor, in a uniquely meaningful way.

Caroline Kenner: Writer, Witch, and Washington Witchdoctor

Tarot has been my day job for the last decade through my company, The Fool's Dog. The Fool's Dog is a Tarot and cartomancy app company that has published almost one hundred Tarot, Lenormand, and oracle card decks available internationally and produced under license from artists, authors, and publishing companies, now under group management.

My husband, Jason, is a senior software developer. His elegant and intuitive software frames the electronic cartomancy experience as subtly as the medium permits. We have worked very hard to make our apps second to none.

I have been reading Tarot for fifty years now. It's been a lifelong interest. In 1971 I received my first working copy of Pamela Colman Smith's masterpiece, the University Press edition of the *Rider-Waite-Smith Tarot*. Seeking magic and mysticism has been my life's focus since childhood.

CREATORS' STATEMENTS

My first magical experience was at the age of seven in the College of the Vestal Virgins, in the Roman Forum. By the end of high school, I frequently conversed with trees and understood their perfectly sensible replies, too.

On May 13, 1980, I went into a secondhand bookstore called The Owl, on the Bryn Mawr College campus. There I found a secondhand copy of Doreen Valiente's *An ABC of Witchcraft Past and Present*. Doreen Valiente's works led me onto my path in Witchcraft, a path that I continue to follow today.

In 1984 I found my first Witchcraft teacher, Andras Corban Arthen of the EarthSpirit Community, located in western Massachusetts. By the early 1990s, I was assisting in the struggle for religious rights among Witches and Pagans in the Washington, DC, area. The rich East Coast Pagan scene was just beginning to blossom.

Before The Fool's Dog was more than a glimmer in Jason's mind, I spent two decades working as a professional visionary healer and a teacher of visionary healing methods. I studied for many years with Michael Harner and Sandra Ingerman. Then I taught those expensively acquired lessons to my own community at a far lower cost.

I am a third-degree Witch initiated by Janet Farrar and Gavin Bone in Kells, Ireland. I'm also a member of the Assembly of the Sacred Wheel (ASW) in Georgetown, Delaware, USA. Ivo Dominguez, Jr. of the ASW has been one of my most important teachers. I participated in thirteen precious weekend workshops over the course of twelve years with Dolores Ashcroft-Nowicki. I have received many ceremonies in Cuban Lukumi and Tibetan Buddhism. From 2006 to 2018, I helped organize Sacred Space, a four-day annual conference on magic, mysticism, and metaphysics that is held annually in the Baltimore-Washington area. Over the course of five decades, I've studied diverse magical subjects, including Tarot, Lenormand, and divination.

It is a pleasure and an honor for me to compose the words that accompany Paula Millet's brilliant card images for *Boadicea's Tarot of Earthly Delights*.

OVERVIEW

Tarot Beginnings

This may come as a surprise to many people: Tarot was not originally designed for divination. Tarot decks were originally designed for gambling. The oldest surviving Tarot cards are from the mid-1400s, created in Milan, Ferrara, Florence, and Bologna, in northern Italy.

Tarot's unique new feature: the Major Arcana, twenty-two cards, sometimes called the "Trumps." Trump is a translation of the Italian word *Trionfi*, or Triumphs. Among the earliest Tarots, the Minor Arcana was not illustrated with scenes, like today's Marseilles decks. The Minors were comparable to playing cards, with card numbers indicated by suit icons, and images of people on the court cards.

Playing cards themselves originated in China in the middle of the 800s CE. Gambling games played with cards developed immediately after papermaking and printing technologies made decks of cards widely affordable. The first gambling game played with cards mentioned in a literary source is the Leaf Game, from the Tang dynasty, 868 CE. The earliest known Chinese playing cards already had four suits, each suit representing different amounts of money.

During the early Middle Ages, decks of playing cards designed for gambling spread south and west along major trade routes out of China. Playing cards became popular in the Near East and spread around the Mediterranean Sea into Europe.

The most obvious direct ancestor of European playing cards came from the Mamluk sultanate in Egypt which existed from the 1200s to 1500s CE. The Mamluk decks were similar to Chinese playing cards, but the suits were polo sticks, cups, swords, and coins.

Medieval European city-states did not necessarily welcome gambling with playing cards into their midst. The first European laws banning gambling games played with cards were enacted in 1367 in Berne, Switzerland, and in 1377 in Florence, Italy.

The earliest Tarot decks were hand-painted works of art created for wealthy aristocrats. The oldest Tarot cards still in existence are from the Visconti-Sforza deck, originally owned by the rulers of the Duchy of Milan. Today, those precious cards are owned by art galleries, libraries, universities, and private collectors in many countries.

OVERVIEW

Tarot decks crossed the Alps from northern Italy into Switzerland and France during the Italian wars of the early to mid-1500s. Originally, Tarot decks were not standardized. Regional styles arose as gambling with Tarot became popular in many European countries.

Tarot remained solely a gambling game for several hundred years. Then in 1781, Antoine Court de Gébelin changed the course of Tarot history.

Court de Gébelin was an Enlightenment writer from France. He was an author, a Protestant pastor, a linguist, an occultist, and a Freemason from the same Parisian lodge as Benjamin Franklin. In 1781, Court de Gébelin was struck with a sudden intuition: Tarot was much more than a simple gambling game.

Instead, he suggested that the Tarot was a repository of timeless metaphysical wisdom left to us by the ancient Egyptians. Although hieroglyphs had yet to be translated, Court de Gébelin proposed that the Tarot was a symbol system based on the ancient Egyptian Book of Thoth.

In a chapter of his multivolume masterwork, *The Primeval World, Analyzed and Compared to the Modern World,* Court de Gébelin claimed that Egyptian priests of Thoth had secretly brought the Tarot to Rome. From the Vatican, he explained, the Tarot was taken to Avignon during the era of dual papacies.

Court de Gébelin's associate, the Comte de Mellet, wrote an essay published in the same volume, describing correspondences between the Major Arcana and the Hebrew alphabet. As an appendix, Court de Gébelin included a guide to cartomancy with Tarot.

Court de Gébelin's ideas about an ancient Egyptian origin for Tarot are pure fantasy. It seems likely that Court de Gébelin simply made up this tale to provide his personal inspiration with an impressive pedigree.

While Court de Gébelin was the first to recommend working with Tarot cards for divination, Jean-Baptiste Alliette, writing under the metaphysical pseudonym Etteilla, was the original popularizer of Tarot for divination.

Quite possibly in response to Court de Gébelin's claims, Etteilla published *How to Entertain Yourself with the Deck of Cards Called Tarot* in 1785. Etteilla's book includes upright and reversed meanings for each card, along with suggested spreads of cards. Etteilla was the first professional Tarot reader and the first to design and sell a Tarot deck intended as an instrument of divination.

Etteilla perpetuated Court de Gébelin's fantasy about Tarot's supposed ancient Egyptian origin in his own work. Apparently, the puffery worked.

Later, in the mid-1800s, Éliphas Lévi brought Tarot to further prominence for divination and spiritual work. Starting in 1854, Lévi, a French occultist, published a number of volumes on ceremonial magic that included material exploring the metaphysical correspondences between the Kabbalah* and Tarot cards.

In contrast to the situation in France, Tarot for gambling or for divination was virtually unknown in the United Kingdom prior to 1909. Beginning in 1463, English law prohibited the importation of decks of cards intended for gambling. This ban predates the spread of Tarot from northern Italy into Europe.

And so, the Rider-Waite-Smith (RWS) deck was the first Tarot ever published in England. Produced in 1909 along with its companion volume, *The Pictorial Key to the Tarot*, the RWS was explicitly marketed for occult divination. The RWS was published despite significant interpersonal drama, including sundered friendships and broken oaths, from a lineage of people belonging to secret occult societies.

William Rider was a lithographer and the deck's printer. A. E. Waite, the deck creator and author of the guidebook, was a senior occultist and translator of occult books. He studied Tarot as part of the curriculum taught by the Hermetic Order of the Golden Dawn, a metaphysical lodge in London. Pamela Colman Smith, known as Pixie, illustrated the cards. Pixie was a junior member of the Golden Dawn, a professional artist, and a theatrical set designer.

---

*Note on the spellings of Kabbalah: In most instances the use of Kabbalah refers to the Hebrew Kabbalah. The Christian Kabbalah is often translated as Cabala/Cabbala to distinguish it from the Hebrew Kabbalah and the Western Hermetic Tradition use of the spelling, Qabalah. In this instance, Cabala/Cabbala may be the appropriate spelling for Levi's work since he began as a priest in the Catholic Church but later quit the church to become a ceremonial magician. For the average reader, the spelling "Kabbalah" is probably the most familiar among the various traditions.

OVERVIEW

Some of Pamela Colman Smith's designs for the RWS were inspired by the *Sola Busca* Tarot, created in northern Italy in the mid-1500s. Pixie probably saw photographs of the deck in London's British Library. The *Sola Busca* is the earliest Tarot fully illustrated with scenes in the Minor Arcana.

Ultimately the Rider-Waite-Smith Tarot carries the legacy of multiple creators. The following occultists played a role, whether (or not) they wished to participate in publishing the closely held initiatory teachings of their magical lineages: Kenneth R. H. Mackenzie, A. F. A. Woodford, William Wynn Wescott, Samuel Liddell MacGregor Mathers, Arthur Edward Waite, Aleister Crowley, and Pamela Colman Smith, all of whom belonged or contributed to the Hermetic Order of the Golden Dawn.

Pamela Colman Smith, 1904. Pixie, as she was called, changed the history of Tarot with her art, created in partnership with A.E. Waite. Her deck became the most influential Tarot in history.

https://commons.wikimedia.org/wiki/File:PCS_in_1904_The_Reader_magazine.jpg / Public Domain

Although Waite had sworn a solemn oath never to reveal anything he was taught by the Golden Dawn to uninitiated outsiders, he chose to break that oath when he published the Rider-Waite-Smith deck.

Posterity strongly suggests that Waite's oathbreaking has had excellent long-term results: the RWS is the most influential deck in Tarot history.

Like most modern decks, Boadicea's Tarot *follows the RWS model.*

OVERVIEW

Boadicea the Queen

Boadicea was a queen of the Iceni, a tribe that occupied the territory of present-day Norfolk and Suffolk, during the Roman occupation of England in the first century of the common era. After her husband, Prasutagus, died, Boadicea and her daughters expected to inherit his throne under Roman law. Instead, her sovereignty was ignored.

The Roman authorities annexed the Iceni kingdom and confiscated the properties of the king and all the nobles. When Boadicea and her daughters confronted the Roman authorities, Boadicea was scourged for her demands, and her daughters were gang-raped.

Boadicea bided her time until most of the Roman army was busy suppressing an uprising on Anglesey, off the coast of northwest Wales. Around 60–61 CE, Boadicea led an army composed of the warriors of the Iceni and the neighboring Trinovantes in revolt against the Romans.

Boadicea and her army marched first on Colchester, known as Camulodunum, a Romanized city that had been the Trinovantian capital before the Roman occupation. They methodically razed the city. Then the army moved on to London, known as Londinium, and reduced it to rubble.

Archeologists have found thick layers of burned sediment inside the walls of both cities dating to these events, which were recorded by the Roman historian Tacitus and his contemporaries.

Finally, Boadicea and her army marched on St. Albans, then known as Verulamium, burning and sacking a third Romanized city. By then, the Roman army was able to rally. They moved larger numbers of troops into position to confront Boadicea and her army. The Romans defeated her only by overwhelming force.

Historians at the time estimated that before they fell to Roman legions, Boadicea and her army murdered between seventy and eighty thousand Romans and Romanized people.

They took no prisoners.

To Boadicea, we dedicate this Tarot. Consider yourself warned!

OVERVIEW

We dedicate this Tarot deck to Boadicea's wisdom, assertiveness, and courage.

Paula: In 2013 I reestablished my visual-design business under the name Boadicea Design. I chose her name because she has long been a role model and source of inspiration to me. I relate to her warrior spirit and leadership, not out of a desire for power, but out of duty and necessity. Her bold spirit infuses the deck.

Caroline: In 1973, at the age of sixteen, I learned about Boadicea when I worked as a volunteer excavator on archeological sites organized by the Colchester Castle Museum. I worked on Bronze Age, Iron Age, and Roman sites that summer. I dug carefully into the charcoal level left by Boadicea's burning and sacking of the city. I made a pilgrimage to Verulamium and viewed artifacts from Roman Londinium at the Museum of the City of London.

For four decades, I have been venerating Boadicea as a Heroic Ancestress in my spiritual practice.

By invoking Boadicea's name, Paula captured my attention the moment I saw her vivid artwork and chuckled at her wicked sense of humor. It is an honor to write words to accompany Paula's art.

To Boadicea! With love and devotion.

Boudica and her daughters, by T. & H. Thornycroft (1856–83), Westminster, UK

Photo by Paul Walter, CC BY 2.0, https://commons.wikimedia.org/w/index.php?curid=54793030 Image originally posted to Flickr at https://flickr.com/photos/56889160@N00/8433726848

14 *Boadicea's Tarot of Earthly Delights*

OVERVIEW

Why The Garden of Earthly Delights?

Tarot comprises a complex accretion of visual imagery from many eras and European cultures. There are layers of symbolic meaning in Tarot that date back to its Renaissance-era origins, overlain by newer symbolism from more recent times. It's important to stay current with the Collective Unconscious for the best results in divination.

Tarot art is a specialized niche: the artwork in Tarot cards is perceived intuitively as much as it is understood intellectually. Juxtapositions of design elements bypass literal interpretation and speak directly to the reader below the level of conscious awareness, to the heart instead of to the mind.

Detail from *The Garden of Earthly Delights,* central panel, by Hieronymus Bosch
Jheronimus Bosch 023.jpg, Public Domain, https://commons.wikimedia.org/w/index.php?curid=148017

The title *Boadicea's Tarot of Earthly Delights* references Hieronymus Bosch's *The Garden of Earthly Delights* triptych, owned by the Prado Museum in Madrid, Spain. The work is a depiction of an Earthly Garden of Delights poised between panels depicting Hell on one side and Paradise on the other.

Although no actual components of Hieronymus Bosch's *The Garden of Earthly Delights* triptych appear in the collage illustrations for *Boadicea's Tarot,* the nature of this deck very much follows the spirit of his complex, fantastical artwork.

Tarot encourages us to consider our own fate, and to follow our will in choosing Paradise, Hell, or an Earthly Garden of Delights exquisitely balanced between extremes.

MAJOR ARCANA

An introduction to
The Major Arcana

These cards represent important matters or strong influences.

The Major Arcana comprises twenty-two cards, beginning with The Fool, card 0, and ending with The World, card 21. These cards illustrate the grand themes and the core issues we face in our lives.

Boadicea the Queen has been added as an additional Major Arcana card to represent female leadership and sovereignty. She is the guiding spirit of this Tarot.

There are many upon many occult associations and layers of meaning to be found in the Major Arcana. Traditionally, there is a Hebrew letter associated with each card, drawn from the Kabbalah, and a dedicated path on the Tree of Life. There are various spirits and divinities associated with Major Arcana cards. There are occult systems in which the Major cards have special gemstones, plants, or planets assigned to them, all perceived to carry a similar metaphysical resonance to the card image.

One way to analyze the Major Arcana, drawn from Jungian thought: consider The Journey of The Fool. As card 0, The Fool can be considered the Tarot's protagonist, the ego self. The Fool's Journey takes her through each of the twenty-one cards of the Major Arcana in numerical order, meeting the iconic Tarot characters and proceeding through various archetypal human experiences.

The first seven cards, from The Magician to The Chariot, chart The Fool's Journey immediately after she and her little dog tumble down the steep mountainside. This set of seven cards speaks to mastering important skills of normal human life. On a quest for worldly knowledge, The Fool meets various authority figures, finds friends and lovers, and learns how to operate competently in the world.

Beginning with Strength and ending with Temperance, the second seven Major cards speak about self-knowledge, refinement, and initiation. This part of The Fool's Journey requires strength of character, and the determination to seek joy. Acknowledging that her truth heals her, she works to refine and purify herself. Only then can The Fool arrive at the calm balance of Temperance.

The final seven cards take The Fool past the game of human life toward more timeless concerns. Yet, some wounded parts of The Fool's self are still painfully enthralled. To heal herself, The Fool must acknowledge her problems and act to purify herself of her own limitations. Inspiration from the alchemical Star can elevate, or it can lead to the delusions and illusions of The Moon. The most discerning Fools proceed to The Sun, success and self-knowledge. At the end of her archetypal journey, the now wise Fool is judged favorably by the eternal powers. She moves into the light of The World, with its balanced spiritual attainment in great measure.

B ecause so many different types of magical workers include Tarot in their practices, the Tarot has become one of the richest areas of study in all metaphysics and occultism, a feast of esoterica. If you are intrigued by some of the references mentioned above, you will find that whole books have been written on many of these subjects.

Finally, it is helpful to read with the Major cards alone occasionally. Majors only readings can sharpen our focus on life's most essential issues.

The unexamined life is not worth living.
—Socrates

MAJOR ARCANA

Majors only readings can sharpen our focus on life's most essential issues.

0 | The Fool

A lively lass with the head of an ass is poised at the brink of a cliff. Despite the fearful precipice, she dances joyously, wildly, seemingly oblivious to her peril. Her little dog prances beside her, and a fat bumblebee buzzes across her path. The sky is blue above golden fields far below.

INTERPRETATION:

The Fool blithely embarks upon a new adventure, with good luck as her companion and the world unfolding at her feet.

    Upright: The beginning of a journey, whether literal or spiritual. *Go for it!*

    Optimism, innocence, youthful enthusiasm, new beginnings. Adventure and high spirits. The Fool's cliffside shenanigans and open-hearted *joie de vivre* attract both allies and satirists, inspiring both mockery and happy laughter. The Fool amuses people. Her wild dance on the cliff's edge would be less exciting to observers without the looming danger.

    Humor always has an edge, whether cuttingly cruel or benign. Are people laughing at you or with you? Cuts from comedy's sharp edge, some bee stings, and a few falls off the precipice will eventually teach

motivate The Fool to do what's necessary to transmute her head, and she will become more fully human.

But for now, The Fool's head remains asinine, her dance carefree.

Reversed: Oblivion and ignorance, whether willful or unintentional. Insensitivity, even narcissism. Failure to perform personal shadow work, leading to toxic family dynamics from the past perpetuating and poisoning the present. Refusal to grapple with financial issues, refusal to show up for life.

In reversal, the ill-dignified Fool is unwilling to change, unable to learn from her mistakes. She can become defensive when challenged about her intransigence by people who love her and are trying to help her. Sometimes she will resort to verbal "stings" to cut off such discussions.

At worst, the reversed Fool suffers from depression and alienation.

If this resonates with you, please consider asking for professional help. Depression is a serious illness requiring treatment. Therapy and medication regimens can help people step back from the brink.

Or an ill-fated quest. Please reconsider your plans. Sometimes it's better to nip a bad plan in the bud, before it festers.

SYMBOLS:

- **A bee:** The existential question "To be or not to be?"
- **The precipice:** Risk, adventure, a leap of faith
- **Blue sky:** Optimism, hope
- **A far horizon beyond the mist:** The promise of travels and adventure ahead
- **The head of an ass:** Represents folly and refers to the episode in Shakespeare's *A Midsummer Night's Dream* when Oberon, the King of the Fairies, transforms the head of Bottom the Weaver into that of an ass in order to make a fool out of his wife, Queen Titania
- **The Fool's dog:** Familiar animal guide, the vital animal self, and a faithful companion for the journey

1 | The Magician

The Magician is at work surrounded by the trappings of her craft. She raises a wand and looks over her shoulder to focus on a candle flame. Every surface around her is cluttered with objects both occult and mundane. There are books, globes, skulls, a clock, cards and coins, sheet music, toadstools, a pistol, strings of pearls, a shy squid, a small black bird, a phrenology chart, and a cecropia moth entranced by the flame. The pièce de resistance *is a stuffed armadillo that dangles from the ceiling.*

INTERPRETATION:

Prepare to be dazzled! This virtuoso of improvisation skillfully juggles the very fabric of reality. You might be tricked, or you might be enlightened.

Upright: Here is a person of great power and charisma. Crafting reality through self-knowledge in accordance with will. Ambition, determination, and self-mastery, leading to triumph.

The Magician has all the tools she needs to control herself and the perceptions of others. Her most important tools are deep self-knowledge and radical self-love. She has examined her life. She knows who, why, and how she is herself. The Magician fully accepts all of herself, her strengths and limitations, her loves, her challenges, her brilliance, and her obscurity. She has cast away guilt and shame and gone beyond society's programming. She is capable of the intense concentration and focus that changes the world.

As well as self-mastery, The Magician's tools include command of the four elements, the nine worlds, the stars, and even the cosmos.

She has transmuted herself into an intersection of change in keeping with her will. She has become a pivot point so powerful that time and space rearrange themselves around her.

Use your most exquisite discernment in relation to The Magician, especially if this card represents you.

Reversed: Personal power used to deceive, misinform, or control. An attractive but false glamour. A fast talker, a swindler, a con artist, a grifter. A polished veneer of truth over rough lies, a sugar coating on a poison pill.

The reversed Magician is dangerous. She uses her charisma to smooth her path at the expense of others. She is skilled, ambitious, and free of ethical considerations. Her only concern is fulfilling her needs and desires. She is liable to use psychic attack methods on people she perceives as opponents.

Will your meeting with The Magician be for good or for ill? That will depend on how closely your personal POV and The Magician's POV overlap.

Watch your back.

SYMBOLS:

- **Infinity symbol / lemniscate:** Eternity, limitlessness, infinite possibility
- **Baton or wand:** Power of intention, focusing the will, a link between the spiritual and earthly realms
- Symbols of the elements: **Combustion/Fire:** candle; **Tentacles/Water:** squid; **Æther/Air:** embroidered tapestry wing, blackbird, moth; **Fungi/Earth:** toadstools and an armadillo (which also refers to alchemy)
- Globes: **Mercury:** corresponds to The Magician; **Astrological Sphere:** astrology; **Earth:** the world at the Magician's fingertips
- Vanitas items: **Skulls:** mortality, hidden structure; **Clock:** time passes; **Books and curiosities:** pursuit of knowledge and study of the natural world; **Pistol:** arrogance, force; **Coins and jewels:** earthly riches; **Sheet music, playing cards:** amusements, distractions; **Phrenology chart:** there are many approaches to understanding our minds and characters.

2 | The High Priestess

A mature woman with a knowing expression sits beneath an octagonal temple. She wears a crescent diadem and possesses an hourglass and a scrying mirror. Half of the temple's columns are black marble, and the other half are white alabaster. Pomegranates decorate the frieze.

The High Priestess is perched on the edge of an overflowing spring surrounded by the infinite cosmos. A huge moon floats just within the ring of columns, reflecting silvery light on the pool, the mirror, and the priestess.

INTERPRETATION:

The High Priestess sits at the gate between the mundane and the spiritual realms, between ordinary reality and the Otherworlds, the mythic realms. She's seen it all, and she's nobody's fool. She reveals the intangible and knows the unknowable.

Upright: Deep spiritual knowledge about life, death, and transcendence. Hidden mysteries brought to light. Access to the Collective Unconscious, ability to reach beyond space and time.

The High Priestess sits in a liminal place betwixt and between our world of tangible reality and the invisible worlds. Her temple is a hub, with access to spiritual, etheric realms known to all humanity in various forms.

The High Priestess knows the Gods and Goddesses and many other types of spirits personally. She can consult spirits for the benefit of herself and others, in search of wisdom and healing, in search of knowledge, and to find hidden things. She has the discernment to know which spirits offer responsible counsel and divine healing, which spirits are working to help humanity—and which spirits are better off left alone.

The High Priestess possesses all the psychic gifts. She is a Mantis, in the ancient Greek meaning of prophet, soothsayer, oracle, diviner. She is a trance priestess, a necromantic medium who lends her voice to the Ancestors, loving spirits, and the Gods themselves. She is a healer, a bard, a diviner, sometimes an oracle, and oftentimes she takes all of those roles.

Gaze deeply and keep an open mind.

Reversed: Do you have night terrors for no apparent reason?
There is no place to hide from the spirits. If you are receiving a call from the spirits and trying to ignore that call, you do so at peril to your physical and mental health. You would be best advised to answer sooner rather than later, for your own sake.

Or, are you trying to hide your own underlying motives or emotions? Perhaps it's time to acknowledge your murkier side, at least to yourself. The truth will come out eventually, with or without your help.

SYMBOLS:

- **The moon:** The occult revealed, light reflected back out of the darkness
- **White and black columns:** Duality; Light/dark, good/evil, truth/deception, known/unknowable: the Priestess is neither one nor the other, but in between all.
- **Pomegranates:** Refer to the mythology of Demeter and Persephone
- **The dark and formless void:** The cosmos, infinity
- **Upwelling pool:** The Source
- **Mirror (or cosmic tablet):** Scrying, second sight, portal for cosmic wisdom
- **Hourglass:** The endless cycle of time

MAJOR ARCANA

3 | The Empress

Crowned with ginger fritillaria flowers, this imperial lady holds herself proudly, with a direct gaze and a regal bearing. She rests on a marble bench in front of an open window, with a vista of her castle and great estate.

The Empress is wearing a lavish gown of gold and silver brocade, with a collar of Madonna lilies, and a skirt draped with pitcher plants buzzing with colorful insects. A jewellike hummingbird perches upon her outstretched hand.

INTERPRETATION:

The Empress embodies the fertile and nurturing powers of Mother Nature. She is Divine Nature herself.

Upright: Creative and procreative power. Fecundity and abundance. Physical motherhood, or supportive help that nurtures and heals coming from someone else. Living in harmony with the earth.

Acknowledging the soul shared by all beings, including the planet itself. The Gaia theory. Goddesses, especially such as Artemis with dominion over the wild places, or such divinities as Lakshmi and Freyja, who embody prosperity and fertile abundance.

Here, Divine Nature is embodied as a female monarch. The Empress is shown in majesty as the Creatrix and the Nurturer, her domain the manifest world. Her powers of procreation are truly titanic, like Gaia herself. She is the power of earthly fertility, the giving mother, the loving nurturing powers of the divine feminine. Her beauty, her youth, shows us what society most values in women: women are considered the most powerful when young, beautiful, and nubile, ready to bear children.

In our era, humans are finally beginning to find ways to work in partnership with nature, as we edge ever closer to severe climate disruption. Until human attitudes toward the manifest world change, we will continue to destroy and degrade the world. Our planet is not a storehouse of raw materials designed for human use. Nature is possessed of soul and has intrinsic value far beyond money.

Reversed: Motherhood gone awry. Failure to nurture. Denial of maternal love, lack of care; at worst, neglect or even abuse. Cruelty to children and animals.

Polluting or abusing the earth. Profiting from pollution, tolerating polluting practices, or concealing polluting practices from inspections. Abusive agricultural practices, use of poisonous agricultural or industrial chemicals. Environmental destruction.

The shadow side of The Empress sometimes speaks to a serious loss of vitality, or a debilitating illness.

The Empress reversed suggests Goddesses similar to Kali, The Morrigan, Hel, or Persephone as Queen of the Dead.

SYMBOLS:

- **Flowers:** Fecundity, fertility, femaleness
- **Crown Imperial (fritillaria):** The Empress's crowning glory, majesty, power, arrogance, pride of birth (note: this Empress is a redhead)
- **Castle:** Ruling status, earthly riches, security and power
- **Madonna lilies:** Blessed motherhood, purity
- **Hummingbird and insects:** Pollination, conception, reproduction, "the birds and the bees"
- **Pitcher plants:** Carnivorous vessels, womb-like in appearance, representing a life cycle where flesh ingests flesh and flesh begets flesh

4 | The Emperor

His Imperial Majesty stands confidently upon a dais regarding his assembled subjects. He is a mighty presence, glowing green and gold against an evening seascape. The royal head is represented as a proud, arching asparagus stalk, bearing a heavy crown. His robes are pearl, richly filigreed with gold embroidery. He wears a sparkling collar of fresh grapes, wields a ceremonial blade, and grasps a lesser stalk of asparagus symbolizing his temporal power.

Like a sprouting horsetail, or a lettuce plant bolting to seed, asparagus shoots have long symbolized male sexual prowess in myth and legend. The Emperor's display of masculine sexual prowess, vegetable style, is reminiscent of the ancient Egyptian Moon God Min, whose sacred plant was a bolting lettuce, with its enormous and rapidly growing stalk.

INTERPRETATION:

A powerful father figure, The Emperor wields legal and political authority. He has never stopped believing in the Divine Right of Kings: he has simply fallen silent on the issue.

Upright: Good Daddy. Benevolent authority. Power tempered by wisdom and compassion. Reasonable laws, benign oversight, equitable policing free of bias, military employed as peacekeepers more than warriors. At best, The Emperor provides good governance, with fair laws fairly applied. He levies reasonable levels of taxation, which he uses to maintain a peaceful civil society in exchange for obedience to his laws.

In the workplace: A strong but fair CEO or CFO, a good manager.

In a family, The Emperor is a strict but kind parent, able to listen to his family. Rules are made clear to all family members and are enforced equitably. Monies are shared justly and fairly among family members. There is a balance between firm rules and an appreciation that life is not a one-size-fits-all affair.

Reversed: Bad Daddy. Misuse of authority. At worst, the reversed Emperor is a demagogue and a dictator. Tyranny. Police state. Stifling, entrenched Byzantine bureaucracy composed of do-nothing parasitic cronies.

In society: Laws applied to impoverished wrongdoers only, while wealthy criminals bribe authorities to drop all charges. Laws applied with racist, religious, anti-LGBTQIA, or political bias. Crimes against humanity. False imprisonment, jailing or assassinating political rivals, cruel and unusual punishment. A corrupt judiciary.

In a family: Forcing children to struggle for autonomy even into adulthood, manipulating family members by giving or withholding money, expecting everyone to defer to them. In an individual: inability to listen to family members, combined with an expectation that all children will live up to identical rules. Regimentation, rigidity of thought, "my way or the highway" black-and-white thinking.

In the workplace: Demands for unquestioning loyalty, and total subservience. Requiring all employees to be fawning sycophants or lose their jobs. Departmental turf wars at the expense of joint projects.

SYMBOLS:
- **Asparagus stalk**: Nobility, authority, prosperity, male potency, a phallus
- **Numerous asparagus berries**: A little pollen goes a long way
- **Grapes**: The fruit of the earth, abundance, transformation and fertility
- **Admiring minions**: Political power

5 | The Hierophant

It is twilight in the forest. The Hierophant approaches. He has a man's body with the head of a mighty stag, wearing white robes and offering a sacred libation. An ethereal ball of light hovers at his crown.

INTERPRETATION:

This Hierophant is an ancient spirit of Divine Nature, an ambassador of Nature's Spirituality. He is a spiritual guide who leads us toward harmony with the soul of Planet Earth.

Upright: A wise spiritual leader. An ethical priest who walks their spiritual talk and leads by example. A dedicated emissary on a mission for spirits and ancestors, or a teacher or priestess helping others find harmony within and without.

Curated enlightenment along a guided path. At best, such seekers go through a series of initiatory experiences, led by elders motivated to spread love and compassion through shared transformative spiritualities.

A nurturing spiritual community. A group of coreligionists walking similar paths as peers in support of one another. Religious beliefs and practices seeking cocreative alliance with divine nature. An understanding that Planet Earth has soul, that animals and plants have soul, and that even rocks, clouds, and stars have soul. Deep faith in the intrinsic value of nature, far beyond any monetary concerns.

Spiritual growth, the ability to transcend one's own limitations. Moving beyond petty hatreds or fears toward serenity, inner peace, and compassion for all beings. Kindness and goodwill.

Reversed: A false priest leading people along a destructive spiritual path. A hate-monger posing as a pastor, preaching human politics, hellfire, and damnation to manipulate his parishioners through guilt and fear. A con artist posing as a priest, manipulating the gullible for financial gain.

Spiritual or sexual abuse of the laity. Exerting religious dominance to exploit congregants. On a personal level, this reversed Hierophant can speak to a crisis of faith. Sudden insight about conventional spirituality, its limitations, and its failures. Surprising perception about the nexus of organized religion, money, and human ambition.

At worst, a cult leader, someone who has weaponized faith so they can attain money and prestige. Corrupt or even criminal behavior by a priest or priestess. Mind control, even brainwashing, designed to instill hate and fear, and often combined with sexual and financial abuse.

SYMBOLS:
- **Stag:** Spirit of the Forest, protector of other creatures, primeval male earth spirit, the Horned God
- **Glowing ball of light:** The cosmos, infinite mysteries
- **Anointing vessels:** To hold consecrating oils
- **Woods:** The forest primeval
- **Twilight:** A betwixt and between time

6 | The Lovers

A man and woman embrace on a garden bench. Sitting upon the man's lap, the woman gazes at the viewer with a bemused expression. She holds a white dove to her throat. The man has turned away from her. He is entirely distracted by a flamboyant woman posing naked between a pink rosebush and tall hollyhocks. She has a "come hither" expression, while playing seductively with her hair.

In the background, the statue of a priapic satyr overlooks a hedge maze. And, curiously, an apple has rolled under the bench.

INTERPRETATION:

Relationships, whether romantic or not, require us to make choices. Choose your partner(s) wisely, in business, friendship, and love.

Upright: A long-term committed partnership in business, leisure, or love. A harmonious and mutually beneficial union that creates synergy for everyone involved. A sudden challenge to a long-standing relationship between peers. New and unexpected options present themselves.

As exciting possibilities present themselves, what are your reactions, needs, and desires? Will your partner(s) react to this new situation in the same way? How will an attractive new possibility affect the existing relationship(s)? How well is your partnership serving you? In a long-term relationship of trust, it is vital to discern sweetly faithful doves from possible vipers nursed at your bosom.

The best way to provide a good foundation in business, friendship, or love is to give your partner(s) good value—and to make certain that your partner(s) are upholding their parts of the bargain as well.

Sometimes this card indicates romantic love, or a new and enjoyable platonic relationship. But those meanings are more often carried by the Two of Tentacles.

Reversed: An unhappy relationship, whether the relationship is platonic, romantic, or a business partnership. Betrayal of trust. Discord that undermines people's ability to work as a team.

Sexual jealousy, whether justified or as a product of insecurity. Envy of another couple's happy relationship, or envy aroused by a friend's financial situation. A friendship that goes sour. Inability to be happy for others' success.

There can be a strong temptation to wish that Miss Naked would step into the prickly pink rosebush and get scratched by thorns. However, in long-term relationships, there is always going to be some Miss Naked or other, coming down the pike to offer themselves as a possible alternative to current arrangements.

Pay attention to Mr. Cozy Lap and his reactions now, and not to Miss Naked in all her seductive flamboyance.

SYMBOLS:

- **Garden:** Fertility cultivated and controlled
- **Satyr statue:** Lust
- **Dove:** Purity
- **Hollyhocks:** Ambition
- **Pink roses:** Sensuality, happiness
- **Painted lady butterfly:** The fleeting moment, metamorphosis
- **Hedge maze:** Earthly manifestation of the labyrinth concept, making decisions to find your true path; will Lust be a guide to that true path?
- **Apple:** The fruit of knowledge of good and evil, giving in to temptation, Eris's golden apple of discord

7 | The Chariot

Standing on the surface of the moon, a charioteer struggles to control two powerful horses. He is nude but for a scarlet drape. His muscular body glows blinding white, and a golden wheel surrounds his dark head.

In the distance, ancient Egyptian pyramids and the Sphinx rise above the lunar horizon. The faraway stars and a gibbous Earth hang in the black velvet of space.

INTERPRETATION:

Life hurtles along willy-nilly, but the Charioteer can control even the strongest, most-passionate horses. He harnesses his team and navigates a steady course through every transformation and challenge.

Upright: Road trip! Wherever you are going, you are moving quickly, and in the right direction. You have set irrevocable events into motion, and you are making progress toward your goal.

You are your own best tool. You are in control of your destiny in exact proportion to your ability to harness yourself and manifest your goals, even in the face of rapid change. The Chariot is controlled by the Charioteer's fine degree of self-mastery combined with discipline and skill. Rapidly changing circumstances demand focus and concentration for The Chariot to remain on course.

The Chariot forcefully makes its way through the waves of time, manifesting change in its wake. The Charioteer's self-mastery gives The Chariot powerful positive momentum. His momentum sweeps away all opposition: he and his team bring forth widespread influence in accordance with the Charioteer's will. Develop your will, work on increasing your concentration, and The Chariot says you, too, will meet your goals.

Reversed: Beware Cosmic Potholes! Are your efforts stalled temporarily or sidelined for the foreseeable future? Delays, diversions, and distractions are hindering progress.

Time is a-wasting: taking steps toward improvement cannot wait indefinitely for a more opportune moment. How can you get beyond the current obstacles to your progress? How are you sabotaging yourself?

Or are you rushing thoughtlessly along, barely under control, failing to focus, ignoring important details . . . and thereby bringing future problems
into being? Whoa, slow down, breathe, and take things more slowly.

Anxiety can spur people into making decisions too quickly. Hold yourself gently: master your emotions, take your time, consider your options carefully, and make your decisions accordingly. You'll have better outcomes in the longer run.

Be realistic. If a project is not manifesting the results you had hoped for, ask yourself if it's time to drive on.

SYMBOLS:

- **Wild horses:** Could drag you away, opposing powers requiring conscious control, self-mastery, harnessing power to create results
- **The moon:** Its orbit of the earth is a balance of gravity and momentum; success is often driven by emotional states
- **Wheel:** The Wheel of Fortune: incessantly turning forward
- **Constellation of Auriga, the Charioteer:** Is fate truly written in the stars?
- **Egyptian ruins on the moon:** Well, one never knows . . .

8 | Strength

A serene young woman looks on at a small white lamb surrounded by four big cats. Despite the threat of mortal peril, the lamb is completely fearless, even cheeky, as it stares them down.

The woman is so unperturbed that she rests against the lion's flank. Any thought of danger is an illusion. She has complete control of the situation.

INTERPRETATION:

Strength triumphs over brute force gently, with love and compassion.

Upright: Trust yourself. You have achieved a fine degree of inner harmony and balance resulting in personal strength. The upper self and the middle self kindly master the lower self and befriend the shadow self to create a unified self. When our will, our emotions, our rational mind, and our instincts are held in balance with compassion, we are able to act from a place of great strength and power.

Self-mastery is best approached gently. Personal healing work includes controlling our own violent or self-destructive tendencies and negative states of consciousness, using a combination of rational thought, patience, and love.

Inner harmony manifests as strength of character: the patience and endurance necessary to face life's challenges with courage and resilience.

Reversed: Brave heart now.

When gnawing anxiety and fear for the future are overwhelming, it's time to sit down and breathe. Whether the crisis is caused by outward circumstances or by inner turmoil, it's best to engage your rational mind and problem-solve, instead of panicking.

What can you personally do, something that you believe you can do long term, that will alter the dynamic between you and the source of your fears?

In this life, the only being we can really control is ourselves. Outward circumstances definitely change in response to inner healing, however, in accordance with the saying from the Emerald Tablet attributed to Hermes Trismegistus: "As above, so below, as within, so without, to accomplish the one work."

Manifesting the strength of character to make long-term life changes takes patience and self-discipline. Hold yourself calmly but firmly to your goals. Forgive yourself when you fall short, and move past the mistake quickly, having learned from it. You will survive to thrive thereby.

Think of it as weight training for your willpower.

SYMBOLS:

- **Twin shields:** Feminine power and endurance, nurturing and forbearance
- **Infinity symbol / lemniscate:** Eternity, limitlessness, infinite possibility
- **Big cats:** Powerful impulses and emotions, physical strength, predatory urges
- **Lamb:** The power of pure intentions, (classically) innocence
- **Peacock feathers:** A bird sacred to the Goddess Hera, its feathers evoke the many eyes of Argus, her never-sleeping watchman

9 | The Hermit

A man wearing a magical hat sits by a wide-open window, looking onto a frozen landscape. He appears to be in a meditative state. His humble quarters hold a single chair, a lantern, a wooden staff, a basket, and a modest repast.

Outside, in the distance, a ship is trapped in ice. Will the stranded mariners see The Hermit's lantern light through the open window?

INTERPRETATION:

Find a quiet place. Look deeply within yourself to light the wise Hermit's lantern in your own heart.

Upright: The unexamined life is not worth living.

Open your heart and mind to spiritual guidance, whether it comes from inner promptings, human teachers, or omens from nature.

It's time to isolate yourself from the distractions of daily life as best you can. Is there is a gentle inner voice vying for your attention, hoping you will listen? Amid the hurly-burly of everyday existence, it is difficult to hear our own inner voices. Our modern world downright encourages us to ignore such inner promptings. But if we fail to listen to those inner voices, our lives can become superficial, an endless routine of work interspersed with consumerism, leisure, and sleep.

Ask yourself: Who am I? What roles can I play, how can I serve the descendants' best interest, what can I personally do that will improve the future?

Spiritual discernment arises with a wider perspective. A mixture of learning from human teachers, listening for those small inner voices, reading books, performing divination, and watching carefully for those synergistic "coincidences" we call omens, all together will enable enormous spiritual progress.

This is how people advance to become full spiritual adults, taking responsibility for their actions and reactions on every level of existence. This is the path of direct inspiration from the Divine.

Reversed: The unexamined life is a shallow affair. Ceaseless distractions delay much-needed self-reflection.

Are you satisfied with skating along the icy surface of human life? Are you denying yourself the heights of being human by refusing to plumb your inner depths? Many upon many people ask for no more from life than a cycle of work, leisure, consumerism, sleep, repeat. Discernment begins with truthful self-analysis.

When people are shipwrecked and trapped in ice, it's best to walk toward the lantern light shining through the distant window.

SYMBOLS:

- **The Arctic:** There is purity in deep cold and ice
- **Ship frozen in ice:** Isolation, stasis, and entrapment
- **Open window:** Looking out on the world from within one's self
- **Lantern and staff:** Seeking the truth, Diogenes the Greek Cynic philosopher in his search for an honest man
- **Three fish in a bowl:** A trinity, the power of three

10 | Wheel of Fortune

Symbols abound in this image. An ancient bronze wheel, the central element, bobs on ocean waves. Various creatures surround it: a monkey holding a skeleton key and an apple while riding a lobster, a blue serpent entwined in the spokes, and a mournful owl squatting on an octopus. A dark-winged sphinx clutches the wheel's rim. A dove and a bat circle her head. The scene unfolds before a ruined city behind a wall of flame. Jupiter fills the sky, bisected by a rainbow.

INTERPRETATION:

Change is Fortune's only constant. What fate have you pursued? Tomorrow is another day; tomorrow offers another chance.

Upright: Good luck and good times. *Laissez les bons temps rouler!*
When The Wheel turns in your favor, it can be intoxicating. As we ascend in a progressive cycle, bringing benefits such as financial security, success in love, happy partnerships, good health for ourselves, and strong healthy children, it is easy to forget that there will be an inevitable fall after our rise. If we are lucky, the inevitable fall is from the cold wind of time and age, diminishing our abilities one by one, dimming our vitality as we slide toward our deaths. This is luxury, living to be diminished by age, not dying by disease or cruel circumstance.

Implicit in the ascending cycle is a warning. Beware the intoxication of riding an ascending Wheel. Personal success can lead to the delusion that the cycle will always be expanding, leading to greater growth and more profits in an endless upward spiral.

Yet, for all of Jupiter's powerful abilities at expansion, eventually Saturn will enter the picture, and a downward slide of contraction will arrive, as it has done in endless repeating cycles.

Wise people do well to remember that descents come after ascents, that contractions follow expansions, and that endless growth cycles are illusory.

Reversed: "Are bad luck and hard times dragging you down?"

Sometimes we feel like we are mired into a trough, that a persistent downward spiral of constant struggle is our destiny. At such times, the only way forward is through some sort of change. When we falter or get stuck, best practice suggests we examine our own limitations. How can you work around your limitations? How can you emphasize your strengths? Be coldly realistic.

Being rigorously truthful to ourselves now generally lessens unpleasant consequences (as symbolized by the sphinx) later.

SYMBOLS:

- **Big Wheel:** Keeps on turning
- **Dove:** A messenger of hope
- **Bat:** Night, chthonic realm, necessary for balance—not negative or frightening
- **Sphinx:** The riddles of fate, treacherous and merciless, offering opportunities and pitfalls galore
- **Serpent:** Striving for balance at the apex of The Wheel's cycle; as you rise, so may you also fall; dexterity and adaptability
- **Monkey, Apple, and Key:** Humankind tends to believe that we keep the keys to discerning good and evil, but we are also firmly seated within our animal natures

- **Owl:** Conventional wisdom. Its painful talons grip the octopus' head.
- **Octopus:** Alternate forms of intelligence and ways of thinking, mental flexibility.
- **Lobster:** The submerged mind, the primitive parts of humans shared with many other animals
- **Jupiter:** Planetary association of the Wheel of Fortune
- **Ruins:** "My Name is Ozymandias, King of Kings! Look on my Works, ye Mighty, and despair!" (from *Ozymandias* by Percy Blysse Shelly). Eventually, in all cases, nothing shall remain of us and our lives. Will this be an inspiration, a spur, a challenge, or grounds for despair to you?

11 | Justice

Justice stands in a desert canyon, splitting the sky with the shaft of her spear, held point downward. The left side of the sky is inky black behind a lightning strike; the right side clears to blue behind white clouds.

Justice has the head of a falcon, blindfolded by a feathered hood. She is clad in bright armor with a sword sheathed at her side. Her right hand holds a scale balancing fire and stone, fog and sea.

A pale cobra lies coiled at her feet.

INTERPRETATION:

Although she is blindfolded, Justice sees the truth with total clarity. She is always on the watch, never sleeping.

Upright: Mercifully, you will get exactly what you deserve. Actions have consequences. Natural and human laws determine the balance between mercy and severity.

When people hold true to their finely tuned code of ethics, the consequences of their actions almost always turn out better in the long run. Ethical people uphold ethical boundaries without needing oversight from law enforcement. Unfortunately, this high ethical standard is difficult for some people to achieve.

Justice requires integrity, good judgment, and impartiality. However, the law is not always applied justly in our world. A legal system that strives for fairness even as it constantly falls short is the best we can achieve currently.

Tragically, many people receive only as much Justice as they can afford. People who have done no wrong find themselves mired in dangerously unjust situations. Even when Justice is upright, it may still need to be further balanced by Judgment, Divine Judgment.

Reversed: With severity, you will get exactly what you deserve. Actions have consequences. Natural and human laws determine the balance between severity and mercy.

Have you held true to your finely tuned code of ethics? Have you held true to basic principles, such as Tell the Truth and No Stealing? The consequences of ethically impaired behavior range from none, to social disapproval, and on to prosecution, conviction, and prison.

Carefully consider past actions resulting in disputes, and tell the truth to yourself about your own behavior. How would you evaluate your behavior from an outside perspective? From your opponent's perspective? Try to be impartial.

Or worse, are you being victimized in a miscarriage of justice? Justice reversed will be balanced eventually by Judgment, Divine Judgment. Judgment prevails when no justice is available on the human level.

SYMBOLS:
- **Stormy and sunny skies:** Darkness and light
- **Downward-pointing spear:** Mercy before Severity
- **Empty desert:** The existential plane
- **Arid climate:** Free of the water element, which symbolizes emotion
- **Hooded hawk:** Justice is blind
- **Joan of Arc's armor:** The Armor of Righteousness
- **Scales of Justice:** How one's fate is determined
- **Fire and stone, fog and ice:** Elements in balance
- **Cobra:** Ammit, the ancient Egyptian devourer of unworthy souls

12 | The Hanged Man

A two-faced man hangs upside down from a massive tree. One face contemplates the large egg that he holds; the other face watches a passing wolf. He wears two red Phrygian caps with dangling gold tassels, which are reflected in the turquoise pool beneath the trees.

Two ravens perch by his sides, while a third looks down from a high branch.

INTERPRETATION:

Sacrifice is often required in life, whether to achieve enlightenment or merely to keep the wolf from the door. The Hanged Man endures his suspension willingly. In his own time, he will right himself—or not.

Upright: You are at the crossroads, the hinge of a decision. A change in perspective may lead to deep insight. Consider carefully and look around yourself now.

The Hanged Man sees rationales for more than one possible choice, as he looks forward and back from his inversion. But yet he lingers, suspended, for now. He is of two minds about what comes next, so he hesitates on the threshold.

This Hanged Man invites comparisons to Janus, a Roman God with two faces who guarded liminal places, places that are neither here nor there, but somewhere in between. The red Phrygian caps are symbols of freedom and liberty. This Hanged Man is consciously aware of his inner struggle. He realizes there are arguments supporting both sides of a consequential life decision. As of yet, he is hesitant to act.

The two ravens recall the suspension of the Norse God Odin. Odin's ravens are named Huginn and Muninn, which translate to Thought and Memory. Wise people think about all possible options and consider the background of the situation when making fateful decisions.

In addition to Thought and Memory, there is a third raven, looking down from a high branch. This is the raven Prudence, the annoying but necessary raven of Common Sense.

Reversed: Who is lying to you, and what are they trying to achieve? Or are you lying to yourself?

Are you missing out on good opportunities while you dither at the crossroads? Declining to commit while splitting in half is a decision in itself, but not a functional one.

Are you giving your emotions too much weight in your decision-making, while undervaluing rational thought, or vice versa?

Watch out for tricksters. They enjoy misleading indecisive people at the crossroads. Accepting advice from a conniving wolf pursuing his own agenda is the act of a gullible mark.

SYMBOLS:

- **Tree:** World Tree, cross, or crossroads, where sacrifices are made and destiny is decided
- **Three ravens:** Huginn (thought), Muninn (memory), and their pal Prudence (common sense)
- **Two faces on one head:** Janus, Roman god of duality and doorways, simultaneously looking into both the future and the past
- **The Cosmic Egg:** Total potential; the source of all being, precursor to the Big Bang, the moment before time and space burst into being, the first moment of destiny
- **Wolf:** Big and bad, a threatening warrior or a devil, poverty, fear, deeply entrenched illusions about personal limitations
- **Still water:** A mirror, an inverted reflection of normal reality
- **Phrygian cap:** associated with freedom and liberty

13 | Death

An arch frames a portal in a gray stone wall. Before the arch, a softly glowing stag skull hovers. Beyond, the arch opens onto the star-studded cosmos. The sky is pitch black above the stone wall, with ghostly fingerlike branches reaching upward.

A green luna moth flutters between the antlers of the skull.

INTERPRETATION:

Death is a portal; death is transmutation; death is both a sad ending and a glorious adventure. All cycles end in death, and all cycles begin with transcendence.

Upright: The end of one cycle and the beginning of another. News of a death, or a foretelling of a death yet to come.

The death in question may be the end of a time period, a relationship, or another type of nonphysical ending, or the actual passing of a dear one.

Transformation, transmutation, transfiguration. Even the antlered stag, in his glorious vitality and immense strength, falls to Death eventually. Here, his skull has been bleached bare by the passage of time.

A fuzzy caterpillar goes into a chrysalis and seems to die, only to emerge as a magical being with gorgeous green wings. All is ephemeral; all is passing; all life is as evanescent as a pale moth flitting in moonlight.

The arch opens onto mystery, onto eternity, a time with no time, a place with no physical reality. The stone wall forms a boundary between the living and the dead.

Whether we call it the Land of the Ancestors, Paradise, Heaven, the Elysian Fields, the Duat, or Avalon, the many realms of the dead imagined by humans always have boundaries around them to protect the living by safely containing the dead. This boundary takes many forms, sometimes a river, sometimes cold iron, but whatever the form, the boundary between the living and the dead is always very strong, but not entirely insurmountable.

Out with the old, and in with the new.

Reversed: Stagnation. Refusal to grow, refusal to step into maturity, refusal to contemplate much-needed change. Intransigence.

Depression, or even suicidal ideation. A mental state described by Death reversed requires outside help. If this card describes you, please consider contacting professionals to help you find healing.

On a physical level: coma, life support, ventilator, or a stroke that grossly impairs but does not kill. Alzheimer's or other dementia.

SYMBOLS:

- **Skull of a wild stag:** Physical mortality, mystery, power of regeneration
- **Stone archway:** Gateway between our world and the beyond
- **Bare branches and fallen leaves:** The natural cycle of life and death
- **Luna moth:** Transformation of the soul

14 | Temperance

An angelic woman with wings outspread balances gracefully in the prow of a canoe. Floating on a shallow pond, golden lotus blossoms surround her, rooted in fertile mud, glowing brightly in the sunshine.

The angelic being wears a translucent gown, with a clock face on her halo. Resting one hand atop her head, she is inspecting a goblet of red wine.

In the distance, low-lying land rises up to meet the blue horizon.

INTERPRETATION:

Temperance calls upon us to live a balanced life.

Our time here is finite. Make the most of every moment you are given, and seek moderation in all things, including moderation.

Upright: Temperance is in a fluid state, always shifting and changing to maintain equilibrium.

You walk a golden path of balance. Self-knowledge and self-understanding leading to personal integration. Patience and wise choices result in good health, harmony, and wisdom.

Walking a golden path requires self-awareness combined with a willingness to work steadily toward personal healing. This is how we heal our world: by individual acts of loving kindness and compassion.

Temperance inspires us to examine our personal lives and strive for a moderating balance among our mental, emotional, spiritual, and physical needs. Acknowledging to ourselves that we are suffering or angry or sad as well as courageous and determined to heal is the first step. When we consciously fulfill our needs for nurturance on all four levels of awareness, that is when we have achieved the balance of Temperance.

The most basic level of self-nurturance is the physical. The physical level underlies everything else; mental capacities, emotional sturdiness, and spiritual development all hinge on a healthy body, a body sufficiently robust enough to support our more subtle functions.

Our time here is limited. Walking a balanced path, a golden path of healing, on an individual level is one way we seed a better future, with responsible, loving actions in the present.

You are doing a good job at this important task of personal spiritual evolution.

Reversed: Is your life uncomfortably unbalanced? Is this a result of self-sabotage, or circumstances largely beyond your control? Tell yourself the truth.

Or are you choosing to ignore a problem? Problems almost never spontaneously resolve. Could you possibly be indulging yourself?

Learning to love yourself more deeply, to honor all aspects of yourself, can often heal self-defeating behavior and resolve long-standing pain.

SYMBOLS:

- **Rainbow:** Iris, divine messenger for the Greek Gods on Mount Olympus
- **Clock face:** *Tempus fugit*
- **Goblet:** *In vino veritas*
- **Lotus blossom:** An embodiment of beauty and purity that grows from the mud, spiritual promise
- **Tippy canoe:** Balance
- **Mudskippers:** Amphibious fish that live both in and out of water

MAJOR ARCANA

15 | The Devil

Within a roiling Hellscape, the Devil looms over two puny humans. Although the pair are held by golden chains, their collars are so loose they could easily remove them. These purported prisoners appear to be bickering with each other, undaunted by The Devil and his lascivious lolling tongue.

INTERPRETATION:

You have forged those chains and have chosen to wear them all by yourself. It is well within your power to free yourself, if you choose.

Upright: What do you really want?
   Consider that carefully. This card is a warning.
   Gooey, yummy, irresistible temptation presents itself. Will giving in end in regret? Will self-indulgence in short-term pleasures have long-term bad effects? Addictive behaviors, whether related to substances, obsessions, or delusions, tend to have long-term corrosive effects. Some are able to develop the strength of character to discipline themselves and heal their addictions, but many upon many cannot. Now, The Devil says it is time to reach out for help.
   Using substances or enacting addictive behaviors are ways to avoid resolving leftover pain. Asking for help is often the first step toward healing our deepest inner wounds. There are remedies for suffering; assistance is available for depression and anxiety.

We ignore such inner wounds at our peril. When we suffer from persistent unhealed emotional or spiritual wounds, we have two choices: we can work to heal those places, or we will act from those places. Permitting the least healed aspects of our character to dominate our personalities and take the lead in our lives almost never has desirable long-term results.

Reversed: People erode themselves with self-destructive habits and behaviors. Ongoing addictive behaviors are harmful to life, liberty, and the pursuit of happiness.

The Devil reversed describes a deep dive into self-sabotage, a dedicated commitment to self-destruction, or a determination to remain in a relationship that diminishes self-respect and forbids happiness. Sometimes, this card describes harmful devotion to a false spiritual leader, a Hierophant reversed type. Are you being exploited for money by an unethical priest or spiritual teacher?

No one can help people who will not help themselves. Please consider asking for outside help and begin working to free yourself now.

What do you love about yourself and your life? Start there.

SYMBOLS:

- **Krampus:** The Devil you know
- **(Loose) chains:** Self-imposed limits
- **Bat-kinis:** All the rage in Hell this season; perfect for bathing in flames

16 | The Tower

It is a dark and stormy night. Multiple lightning blasts strike an iconic metal tower. Sixteen black vultures bear witness to the destruction, hoping to pick through the rubble when the dust settles.

Yet, not all is lost; a gaily striped balloon carries escapees swiftly away from the storm.

INTERPRETATION:

Catastrophes, natural disasters, and sudden reversals of fortune happen. Such dramatic upheavals are destructive and very difficult to navigate in the short term.

The fall of The Tower is traumatic. Eventually, a time will come for renewal. The Tower's fall will have cleared the way for those new beginnings.

Upright: Lightning strikes with destructive force. The Tower falls, the status quo fails, and all seems lost.

Tower time is a period of rapid destructive change, when life's accustomed patterns and structures fail. Tower times are very hard to cope with: they are often frustrating and exhausting. However, when lightning strikes, there is nothing we can do to control what happens next. At that point, we are along for whatever ride our fate has in store.

When we bow to overpowering force, the helplessness we feel is very unpleasant. Whatever type of catastrophe, The Tower speaks of an overwhelming experience of sudden loss. A Tower experience divides the past and the future. It is life-changing, a before/after event in memory.

Tower times include suddenly losing a long-held job, unexpected poverty, or the abrupt end to a relationship or marriage. Sometimes, people deliberately create their own Tower times out of desperation for change. Newfound freedom is often obtained at great cost.

What does the Tower's fall teach us? What did the escapees salvage, as they float away from the devastation and rubble?

Reversed: The End. Time to move away now. The Tower reversed is just as final, and just as devastating and painful, as the upright card.

However, sometimes situations that seem very unfortunate, even tragic, in the short term turn out to be mixed blessings in retrospect. Brave heart now. There will be a good next act, a silver lining here.

Or, clinging stubbornly to old thinking, refusing to adapt to changing circumstances. Those are not functional strategies now. Bowing to the inevitable sooner rather than later will save both time and trauma. Circumstances have brought about destruction. Time to deal with it.

Are you making a deliberate choice to remain trapped in the rubble of The Tower?

SYMBOLS:

- **Lightning:** The proverbial bolt from the blue
- **Vultures:** Invaluable scavengers, here to clean up after the disaster
- **Hot-air balloon:** Escape though ingenuity and foresight

17 | The Star

Flaming stars falling from the heavens shower a beautiful naked woman as she reclines at the edge of a waterfall.

Adorned with a starfish in her navel, the woman stretches, confident and free in her luxuriant beauty. She relaxes against two amphorae gushing water both above and below the brink of the waterfall.

A little brown snake lies coiled under exotic plants growing beside the falls.

INTERPRETATION:

Hope. Divine guidance. The Waters of Life. Serendipity.

Upright: After The Tower comes The Star. When all is lost, what remains is Hope. The Star's sparkling light guides us into the future, even during the darkest nights of the soul.

Ad astra per aspera is a Latin proverb. In English, it translates as "To the stars through hardships." Starlight inspires us to remain hopeful and reminds us to keep moving. The Star encourages us to rise above our circumstances, to heal pain and suffering in ourselves and others. The Star steers us toward personal divine guidance and helps us grant forgiveness and find inner peace.

This card carries a mythic theme similar to Pandora and her box. When Pandora released all the ills of the world from her box and slammed it shut, all that remained trapped inside was Hope.

Keeping hope alive in our hearts is essential as we work toward a better future for ourselves, our communities, our local environment, and our planet. There are aspects to modern life that promote despair. We must keep hope alive, even under difficult circumstances.

The Star is considered the most favorable card in the Tarot. When we resonate with the Star, we are flowing with cosmic currents, in harmony with our time, radiant with etheric light, and, often, inspiring others by our example.

The Star inspires people to live lives of joy, and to work toward spiritual evolution. People inspired by the Star set an example and chart a path for many others. This helps everyone take courage and find their spiritual strength, so they, too, may strive for the stars.

Reversed: Do not abandon hope. Do not despair. Keep looking to the stars for inspiration. Keep moving forward.

This is a setback. You will find the right path for yourself. Read the upright meaning carefully.

SYMBOLS:

- **Meteor shower:** Wish upon a shooting star
- **Sea star:** Stella Maris / Aphrodite / Venus
- **Waterfall:** The falling waters mirror the falling stars
- **Protea flowers:** Infinite mutability; Proteus is the Greek god of "sea change"
- **Crocus:** The ability to thrive
- **Snake:** Ouroboros, the serpent that consumes its own tail; infinity

18 | The Moon

The Moon fills a misty chamber, hovering between a staircase and a door. A shallow pool covers the floor. In the foreground a naked woman leans on a plinth, a full moon in her ample curves. She gestures toward the Moon and wears a fiddler crab in her hair.

INTERPRETATION:

Dreams, visions, illusions, delusions. All that is unconscious is the domain of the Moon. Uncertain moonlight reveals a realm obscured, betwixt the waking world and eternity.

Upright: Moonlight is a tricksy form of illumination. Occult forces, spirits, and our own desires can influence our perception more easily under moonlight. It is difficult to distinguish a moonlit path ahead. Wavering moonlight is just as apt to conceal as to reveal.

The Moon's uncertain light illuminates human illusions and fantasies. Sometimes bright moonlight paradoxically outlines delusions or attractively packaged lies. But the Moon also veils divinely inspired visions, epiphanies, and true dreams, sleeping or conscious. True dreams can become goals and, with work, be made manifest.

Dreams and inspired visions take us to ethereal realms of possibilities that comprise that which shall be, that which may be, and that which could be but is not yet. But beware: human ambitions, loves, hates, and fears also color liminal realms on the cusp of manifestation.

The highest level of discernment is required to differentiate human projections, culture specific and otherwise, from the divine or angelic realms. Humans come to grief when they mistake their own cultural or personal preferences for bedrock eternal truths applicable to all humanity. Diligent self-reflection yields the insight and discrimination necessary to disambiguate illusions and see beyond delusions.

Intuition and psychic abilities peak under silver moonlight.

Reversed: Embrace the deepest aspects of yourself. Be honest to yourself about yourself. Ask how you came to be, who you really are, what you truly believe.

Try to appreciate your inner shadows for the stories they reveal about you. Our shadowy aspects exist to teach us.

Are you ignoring inner voices? Are you responding to others from a place of pain? Perhaps it's time to contemplate the triggers that reveal shadow aspects of character. Self-reflection can heal the trauma hidden under self-destructive patterns.

Hold yourself gently in compassion and ask yourself, "How do I really feel?"

SYMBOLS:

- **Secret stairs:** Transition between above and below
- **Closed door:** Hidden things
- **Water:** The tides, the unconscious, the Deep
- **Crab:** The astrological sign of Cancer

19 | The Sun

Lovers embrace in a tulip bed. The Sun bathes the heavens with golden light. Helios, mounted on Pegasus, shoots his arrow from within the solar orb. Plump cherubs frolic gleefully, celebrating with pure joie de vivre.

INTERPRETATION:

Success, joy, pleasure, and new life. Today the world is a sun-drenched garden of delight.

Upright: Be confident!
You have everything you need to succeed in your ambitions. The Sun is shining on you with expansive golden bounty. Bright sunlight gilds you, and you shine. Solar energy brings victory, success, and prosperity to all endeavors.

When the Sun card describes a person, they have the charisma, the drive, and the vitality that people need to succeed in their careers. The Sun's energy motivates us to seek success in our ambitions and create a measure of financial security for ourselves. Financial success brings all the comforts that money can buy.

The Sun also heralds simple bodily pleasures, including being comfortable in our own skins and enjoying mutual love. The Sun reminds us to feel deserving of comfort and pleasure, to remember to love ourselves and our physical human lives.

Turn your face to the Sun and enjoy. A time of bright sunlight is upon you. Relax in the warmth and enjoy the Sun's blessings.

Reversed: The Sun still shines upon you with golden bounty, but to a lesser degree. The Sun reversed heralds some success and happiness, but there are metaphorical clouds dimming the card's brilliance in reversal. What changes in attitude might turn the card upright?

Do you feel comfortable in retrospect with how you have handled the challenges you have faced? Be brave and truthful. Look deeply into your own shadow.

By holding ourselves in compassion while examining our most shadowy aspects in the clear sunlight of our consciousness, we can perceive how and why we limit ourselves. Unlearning self-sabotaging behavior can enable us to leave those metaphorical clouds behind us. In the Sun's bright light, we can dispel our internal shadows.

We all deserve success, pleasure, and the varied joys of incarnation under the light of the Sun.

SYMBOLS:

- **Cherubs:** Joy, birth and rebirth
- **Helios:** The Greek god of the Sun. He is depicted inside the Sun's orb, evocative . . . of a fertilized egg
- **Helios' arrow:** The Sun's rays, golden blessings, generative energy
- **Gold ring:** Romantic love
- **The bee:** A pollinator
- **Tulips:** Love, fame, and kisses

20 | Judgment

An angel with sable wings sounds his trumpet from a Technicolor sky. Beneath him is an enormous mound of human skulls. As souls wake to the trumpet, they thrust their arms upward among the skulls. They stretch their arms toward the angel, imploring, joyous, awestruck.

INTERPRETATION:

The past is prologue.

Upright: As the angel suggests, the Judgment card speaks to divine judgment. Awakening, epiphany, breakthrough. You are telling yourself the truth and are choosing to level up.

Human life presents us with constant ethical and moral quandaries. We live at a time of great social ferment, in diverse societies that no longer share a set-in-stone ethical framework. Yet, many virtues are honored by all human cultures, and lots of vices are commonly condemned too.

When the Judgment card appears, ask yourself how your actions, reactions, and life choices might seem to those spiritual beings who sit in divine judgment upon us when we die.

If you are not comfortable with the answers you receive upon self-reflection, there is no time like the present to begin renovating your life, telling yourself the truth about yourself, and deciding to make stronger, better, more loving choices. Changing your life path requires developing strength of character, something that is its own reward.

We all stand naked in our souls before the Divine when we die. Every nuance of our behavior is well known, and all our acts are weighed and measured by the Divine at the end. A life well lived enables us to reach confidently toward the angel when we hear the glorious sound of that final trumpet.

Wise people choose honorable paths that empower them to stand in both humility and pride at the moment of Judgment, having tried their human best to live good lives according to their society and the tenor of their times.

Reversed: It's past time for any course correction that would improve the outcome of your situation. Be truthful to yourself, acknowledge the obvious, and accept the inevitable consequences. If you do not like what you are reaping, change what you sow.

SYMBOLS:

- **Aurora:** Literally, glowing particles in the magnetosphere charged by the solar wind
- **Gabriel's horn:** A glorious wake-up call
- **Skulls, LOTS of skulls:** Stasis, physicality, the plane of manifest existence

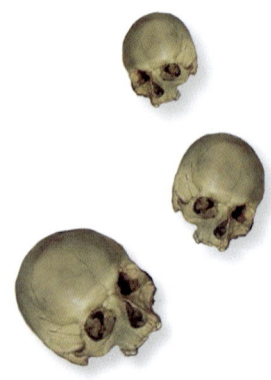

21 | The World

An imperious chimera dances beneath an illuminated vault. Both a beguiling human and an otherworldly octopod, she shakes a tambourine of Planet Earth above her head. With her proud gaze and her curling tentacles, she is entirely self-possessed, both wise and innocent.

Behind her, angels uphold portals to the celestial realms. Creatures representing each of the four elements surround her. The World expresses Spirit, the fifth element that joins all existence.

INTERPRETATION:

*Congratulations! Sometimes we *can* have it all. You have manifested your heart's desire and accomplished your goals! For a few beautiful if fleeting moments, you are dancing on top of The World.*

Upright: Success in great measure, completion of an important life task, victory, graduation, or initiation. Your hard work has paid off, and now you are reaping the rewards. An old cycle ends triumphantly; great effort yields excellent results.

Accomplishment and self-confidence, emotional well-being and spiritual wholeness, good health and a well-balanced life. The World is complete unto herself, perfectly poised and balanced. The breakthrough in understanding described in Judgment has now deepened and becomes integrated in The World.

Because a state of completion is evanescent, The World embodies a transient moment, a pivot point of resolution, before time moves you onward to the next level of challenges. Right now, choruses of angels serenade you. Enjoy your sense of achievement. Your job is done, and well done!

It's time for a lovely celebration, but remember, a new cycle begins promptly Monday morning.

Reversed: Do you feel overwhelmed? When you feel the weight of the world pulling you down, it's time to step back before you burn out. Is too much happening at once? Sometimes we need to dance faster and longer than we are able. Now is a good time to take a break, a rest, even a vacation—or a staycation, relaxing quietly at home.

Longer term, what can you do to lighten your burdens and lessen your responsibilities? What changes could you manifest that would help you achieve your goals?

Ask yourself what is holding you back. Could you be limiting yourself, or are the obstacles to complete success coming from outside you?

You have all the potential, all of the ingredients you need for success already available to you. The World can still be yours with focus, concentration, and a change in perspective. You can turn your situation around so your success can fully bloom.

SYMBOLS:

- **Luna moth:** Air
- **Firefly:** Fire
- **Fish:** Water
- **Snail:** Earth
- **Tambourine/drum:** Beats the pulse of the cosmic dance
- **Tentacles:** Everything is intertwined
- **Cathedral ceiling:** The vault of Heaven

22 | Boadicea the Queen

Boadicea stands in her chariot, with a violent storm brewing behind her. She exhorts her troops to rise up against the Roman Empire. Her two daughters ride beside her, their presence fueling her determination to seek vengeance.

Three corvids circle behind the Queen, symbols of military strategy and battle. The sky roils with crimson storm clouds, evoking the destruction yet to come. Death unfolds in Boadicea's wake.

INTERPRETATION:

In a time of oppression, it is imperative to resist, in order to remain in good conscience with oneself. Rebellion comes as a cleansing when tyrants are overthrown. We owe it to ourselves and our descendants to resist oppression here and now. Silence in the face of institutionalized oppression is consent, even complicity.

Boadicea called upon the ancient Celtic British Goddess of victory, Andraste, for victory in battle. Andraste is similar to Nike in ancient Greece.

Upright: Victory may be inner, a victory over our lower selves, such as commencing a period of sobriety after alcoholism, or external, such as a victory over an opponent or successfully protecting a marginalized person.

Reversed: Boadicea the Queen reversed describes a time when resistance against oppression is necessary, but the inner or outer strength necessary for resistance is lacking.
　　Time to summon your inner and outer resources. Silence in the face of oppression is complicity.

SYMBOLS:
- **Boadicea:** A queen, a military commander, a leader forced into the role by circumstance. The power of women, mothers, and Goddesses. Sovereignty over oneself and one's life.
- **Three corvids:** Strategy, battles, harbingers of war, scavengers of the dead
- **Iceni dwelling in flames:** Destruction wrought by oppression
- **Roman buildings destroyed:** The vengeance of the oppressed and abused
- **Fleeing populace:** War is most harmful to people with the least power. Violent retaliation, even if justified, can unleash unpredictably dire and widespread consequences.

An introduction to
The Minor Arcana

These cards relate to daily life and practical issues.
In a reading they are influenced by any Major Arcana cards.

Four suits, with ten numbered cards and four court cards each, compose the Minor Arcana. In decks such as *Boadicea's Tarot*, inspired by Pamela Colman Smith's images for the Rider-Waite-Smith deck, the numbered Minor Arcana cards illustrate scenes of human life, with portraits of people for the royalty.

While the Majors present grand cycles of archetypal personal evolution, the Minor cards focus on human-level story arcs: people interacting with each other in scenes of human society. The Minor Arcana introduces four story cycles, each illustrating aspects of its elemental energy.

The four suits in Tarot have long been understood to symbolize the four elements of classical Greek thought from antiquity: Wands symbolize Fire, Cups symbolize Water, Swords symbolize Air, and Pentacles symbolize Earth. In *Boadicea's Tarot,* the suit names reveal the elemental qualities of each suit more obviously than in most decks.

Just as there are many layers of metaphysical meanings from many magical traditions for the Major Arcana, there are also innumerable different associations with the Minor cards. Reading the Minors is generally more difficult than reading the Major cards: there are more than twice as many Minors, after all. A deep understanding of the Minor cards and their four narrative cycles enriches readings greatly.

Boadicea's Tarot includes the additional Perspicacious Platypus card, representing self-respect, self-confidence, and whimsy.

MINOR ARCANA

When contemplating the Minor cards as a group, here are some important associations to consider.

The Elements
The nature of the ruling element infuses each card in its suit.

Combustion (Wands) corresponds to the element FIRE, inspiration and energy, as well as hard working, forceful people who are capable of turning ideas into actions.

Tentacles (Cups) corresponds to the element WATER, deep feelings, intuition, emotions and emotional people.

Æther (Swords) corresponds to the element AIR, intellect, ideas and information. This suit represents perceptive, analytical thinkers.

Fungi (Pentacles) corresponds to the element EARTH, material wealth or physical things, and individuals with a practical nature.

The Numbers
Card numbers convey unique flavors of meaning.

Consider numerical interpretations across the four Minor suits. The numbered cards have certain overarching correspondences with each other in the four suits, as well as with the first ten Major Arcana cards.

Each Ace through Ten shares qualities beyond their elemental associations, through their shared number position in the story arc of their suit.

- **Aces** represent the first step in a process, a singleness of purpose, the purest single-note aspect of its elemental association.

- **Twos** carry the concept of duality: a partnership, the joining of a couple, a choice between two options, or the balancing of extremes.

- **Threes** symbolize a trinity: three things uniting in collaboration or teamwork. Dynamic number three can also indicate the third voice needed to unlock a stalemate.

- **Fours** stand for stability, a temporary pause, respite, or plateau, and, sometimes, stagnation.

- **Fives** speak of limitations and challenges to be overcome, or a dynamic situation that may be either improving or deteriorating.

- **Sixes** indicate a period of calm harmony and comfort; chaos has been left behind, for now, at least. Your soul will be nurtured and, perhaps,
your wallet fattened.

- **Sevens** are often considered to be lucky, but in Tarot, Sevens represent unexpected consequences or surprise outcomes, which may be either for better or worse.

- **Eights** stand for accomplishment and thorough understanding, a level both stable and complex.

- **Nines** are the penultimate card in the series, describing a situation that is almost but not quite perfect or resolved. Some individuals are completely content with these situations, and some people can never be satisfied.

- **Tens** signify completion, satisfaction, or ultimate achievement: the climax and The End. Since they mark the fulfillment of a cycle, they also foreshadow the beginning of the next. In some contexts, Tens can represent excess.

The Court Cards
Dramatis personae

The court cards often represent people you know now, have encountered in the past, or will meet in the near future. They provide insight on your significant relationships with family members, partners, bosses, colleagues, and friends. Court cards may also mirror your own character traits back to you.

While real people possess a mix of characteristics, Tarot court cards stand for archetypal personalities or aspects of character. In this context, Tarot's male/female dichotomy is not sexist: it is necessary for organizing the information transmitted in a reading. It's up to the reader or querent to decide what "traditionally" feminine or masculine characteristics
might be.

- **Pages** often represent young people or children, or an older person who is innocent, naive, inexperienced, or simply immature. Pages can also represent the energy and enthusiasm felt at the start of a cycle. Traditionally, Pages are often interpreted as messengers, announcing something that is about to begin.

- **Knights** are active individuals; they go about doing things. They engage in confrontations and rescues and provoke sudden twists of fate. Knights may also indicate a period of intense activity or rapid change.

- **Queens** are mature adults who express a "traditionally female" personality. They may stand for an actual woman, "feminine" aspects of the reader or querent, or the presence or need for traditionally feminine aspects in a situation. Queens symbolize nurturing maternal power. They organize home, family, and community for everyone's benefit. Queens prefer to exert their authority quietly and mercifully, but they will resort to severity if necessary.

- **Kings** are mature adults who exhibit a "traditionally male" personality, a manly man type. Kings can represent actual people, or aspects of the reader's character. Call upon your own ideas of male characteristics and behavior to interpret Kings. Kings invoke paternal power, personal strength, and charisma. When Kings appear in a reading, sometimes there is a need for a more "masculine" approach, perhaps a greater degree of control over the situation, even domination.

MINOR ARCANA

COMBUSTION • FIRE • WANDS • CREATIVE SPIRIT • PURPOSE • WORK • ACTION

Ace of Combustion

From a portal in the great emptiness of space, a human hand emerges from a gilded picture frame. Within the frame, the upper background is obscured by clouds, while the lower background shows a double rainbow. The middle finger has ignited, as the hand reaches past the gilded frame toward the stars beyond.

INTERPRETATION:

First, there is the spark of an idea. Once ignited, this spark cannot be ignored. This card speaks of elemental light and the raw power of creativity, in whatever dazzling form that creativity takes once it manifests.

Upright: Out of the void of space, a hand emerges, a spark ignites a flame, and the flame's light illuminates the darkness.

Let your dreams catch fire! A new and creative endeavor is about to begin. Your path is clear. Take advantage of this opportunity! It is finally time to proceed.

This small flame is so hot and so bright that it will attract helpful allies. Given work, nurturance, and time, you can light a conflagration with one tiny flame.

COMBUSTION • FIRE • WANDS • CREATIVE SPIRIT • PURPOSE • WORK • ACTION

Reversed: Ask yourself how your creativity is being blocked from manifestation.

Are your ideas being thwarted by an opponent? Have you made a solid plan that inspires trust and attracts supporters?

Or could you be tamping down your own creative sparks at the source, by ignoring inner promptings? Make sure you are not getting in your own way and extinguishing your own creative ideas through self-doubt or simple inaction.

SYMBOLS:

- **Hand:** Willpower, the ability to create change, to affect manifest reality by setting events in motion, to nurture an idea into manifestation
- **Flame:** Elemental symbol of the Combustion suit
- **Space:** The final frontier; the vast, dark, silent void prior to manifestation
- **Gilded frame:** Focus, definition, presentation, portal from another realm
- **Double rainbow:** Hope and promise

MINOR ARCANA

COMBUSTION • FIRE • WANDS • CREATIVE SPIRIT • PURPOSE • WORK • ACTION

Two of Combustion

In the privacy of their boudoir, two young ladies conspire over the diagram of a cargo ship. It is night and the moon is full. Through a window behind them, beyond the key on the window ledge, a large ship is consumed by flames. The parchment they peruse glows brightly, backlit by a candle flame.

They both have sly, smug expressions, as if they've realized some kind of advantage. Have they noticed the ship behind them? What does the contract or will underneath the velvet cushion next to them say?

INTERPRETATION:

Business ventures can take unexpected turns. Are your projects practical? Are your plans in order? Will your ship come in, or have all your hopes gone up in smoke?

Upright: You have embarked upon a project and are anxious about the outcome. As you await the results, it still remains to be seen how this situation will play out. If you have worked hard, gathered helpful allies, and planned your project well, you are very likely to succeed.

COMBUSTION • FIRE • WANDS • CREATIVE SPIRIT • PURPOSE • WORK • ACTION

There are differences between theory and practice. Focusing too closely on details while ignoring the business environment around you is unlikely to bring success. And watch your back. Perhaps your partner is promising things they cannot deliver?

Reversed: Expect the unexpected. Do not underestimate the difference between theory and practice. Especially in reversal, this card hints that a controlling focus on small details defeats an entire project. Can changing your perspective further your ambitions?

Is your business is being embezzled, or your creative venture being sabotaged by a partner? Take a good hard look to make sure you are not being swindled.

SYMBOLS:

- **Ships:** Risk and opportunity, hope floats, help is available (but try to ask *before* the ship is on fire next time)
- **Diagram:** Plans, many clever plans
- **Diagram of ship vs. actual ship in background:** Theory vs. practice
- **Key:** Control, boundaries, means
- **Velvet pillow, fancy curtains:** Luxury, wealth
- **Contract or will:** What is hidden about those half-hidden legal documents? Are you sure your interests are contractually secured?
- **Smug expressions:** Are the young ladies taking pleasure in the destruction of a business rival, or are they counting profits that are visibly going up in smoke behind them?
- **The moon:** Secrets either hidden or revealed
- **Illumination close by vs. illumination at a distance:** Differences in focus
- **Framed image of a mustachioed gentleman:** Might someone have a sugar daddy?

MINOR ARCANA

COMBUSTION • FIRE • WANDS • CREATIVE SPIRIT • PURPOSE • WORK • ACTION

Three of Combustion

It is early evening. The dunes near the shoreline are alight with fireflies. Three cloaked figures stand facing the sea, each with a single flame hovering above their identical broad-brimmed hats.
Their gaze is focused upon the vision of a marble palace appearing in the clouds. The details of their shared vision are complete. Now the real work begins.

INTERPRETATION:

You and your partners have reached an accord. Your work is laid out before you, and you are eager to proceed.

Upright: You have found helpful allies in your creative or business enterprise. Your working group has unified, and plans are well in hand.

However, do not permit your eagerness to begin to distract you from the challenges of the path ahead. People who work together toward manifesting a common goal bring their personal limitations with them, as well as their gifts.

Boadicea's Tarot of Earthly Delights

COMBUSTION • FIRE • WANDS • CREATIVE SPIRIT • PURPOSE • WORK • ACTION

Shifting dunes and the sea lie ahead. Both sand and water can extinguish fire. You will experience challenges, crosscurrents, and riptides. You and your partners will need to work through your emotions about money and calculate your willingness to accept risk, while navigating the deep waters that lie before you.

Reversed: At the beginning of creative endeavors, sparks fly freely in a disorganized yet exhilarating way. Review your preparations once again. Confirm shared goals with your prospective partners.

Think deeply and long about your commitment to this project before proceeding.

SYMBOLS:

- **Shifting sands:** An uncertain path
- **Clouds around a castle in the sky:** A magnificent, even grandiose, but as yet unmanifested plan
- **The sea:** Time and tide wait for no one: the sea is unpredictable
- **Identical figures:** A group of people working together on a project
- **The Taj Mahal:** A labor of love, a work of art, a masterpiece of beauty
- **Fireflies:** Inspiration, incandescence, mystic fire, the sparks that lit the three flames

MINOR ARCANA

COMBUSTION • FIRE • WANDS • CREATIVE SPIRIT • PURPOSE • WORK • ACTION

Four of Combustion

In an opulent pavilion, a sensual red-haired woman is enjoying a party for one. She relaxes with tea, fruit, and a handy hookah, while amusing herself with her pet macaw.

Four disembodied arms protrude from the richly decorated walls. Each arm holds a torch, casting a warm glow on her private feast. Through the archway in the background, there is a merry gathering taking place on a moonlit lake.

INTERPRETATION:

Sometimes a relaxing evening at home with your familiar companions is more rewarding than even the most fabulous revels.

Upright: Good fortune! Pleasure and leisure made possible by prosperity and hard work. It's time to celebrate, in whatever way you like best.

You've completed this stage of your work successfully. Time to relax! Now is an ideal opportunity to take a little break and celebrate your success.

People prefer various ways of celebrating. Many people enjoy a good party, while others feel most comfortable with a small number of carefully chosen companions.

COMBUSTION • FIRE • WANDS • CREATIVE SPIRIT • PURPOSE • WORK • ACTION

It's a good time to talk to your allies and consider your next project.

Reversed: If you feel like your achievements are overlooked, ask yourself what you can change, so that your contributions are noticed. Is there a showboat on your team who is stealing the spotlight, or could you be undermining yourself somehow?

Is it time to ask for a raise or look for a different job?

Or are you simply burning yourself out with partying?

SYMBOLS:

- **Palm frond:** Triumph and peace, an end to conflict
- **Salamander:** An elemental being, it dwells in fire but does not burn
- **Hands holding torches:** Active creative abilities made manifest
- **Scarlet macaw:** A large, colorful, and impressive bird, never overlooked
- **A full moon and fresh fruit:** A cycle completed, bearing sweet rewards

COMBUSTION • FIRE • WANDS • CREATIVE SPIRIT • PURPOSE • WORK • ACTION

Five of Combustion

Five snarling hounds attack a stag with his enormous antlers ablaze. The stag defends himself capably. His antlers alone are formidable, apart from the flames. The dogs outnumber him, but he is a brave and resourceful creature, willing to fight on despite the odds.

INTERPRETATION:

A bad day at the office.

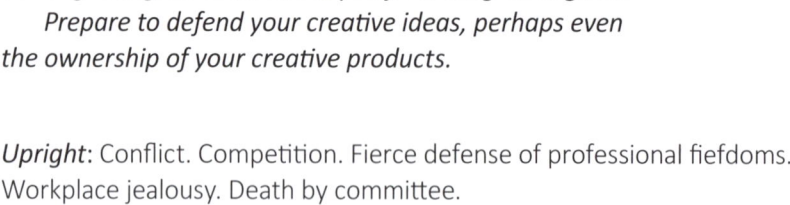

Do not allow a pack of barking mongrels to sidetrack you from long-term goals.

Prepare to defend your creative ideas, perhaps even the ownership of your creative products.

Upright: Conflict. Competition. Fierce defense of professional fiefdoms. Workplace jealousy. Death by committee.

Do not take anyone's claims of good faith on face value here. Watch your back. If success can be snatched from the jaws of these hounds, it will be a minor miracle. Certainly nothing about this situation will be resolved soon.

COMBUSTION • FIRE • WANDS • CREATIVE SPIRIT • PURPOSE • WORK • ACTION

Sometimes, less gifted people wish to undermine creative people out of envy. Other times, people are invested in preserving the status quo because it is familiar, if dysfunctional, or because they have a financial interest.

Reversed: When this card is reversed, the struggle the card describes is less severe than when the card is upright. With the flames at the bottom of the image, with the hounds' legs in the air, success may be hard won, but it is achievable.

Heat rises. The image suggests that the mob's feet will be held to the fire eventually.

SYMBOLS:

- **Stag at bay:** Defensive power, virile energy, regeneration
- **Hounds:** Pursuit and attack, dealing with pack mentality
- **Flaming antlers:** Creative ideas, creative products, skills, knowledge
- **Single stag with a pack of hounds:** A qualitative discrepancy between the abilities of one individual on a team, compared to the others working on the project

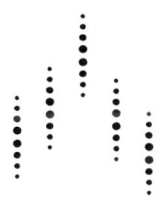

COMBUSTION • FIRE • WANDS • CREATIVE SPIRIT • PURPOSE • WORK • ACTION

Six of Combustion

Two flaming giraffes carry a wise-eyed woman wearing a golden sunflower crown in a triumphal procession. Five adoring maidens cleave a path through a swirling rose petal avalanche. Onlookers dine alfresco, feasting in celebration of her victory.

INTERPRETATION:

Triumph! Success in your endeavors! A jubilant parade! You were right all along!

Upright: You have worked hard. You deserve these accolades. You have earned people's respect, and others look to you as a role model. Your self-confidence blooms; you are proud of your work. You've earned your gorgeous attire, and the flaming giraffes too.

Now that you are successful, the next challenge is to keep your feet on the ground, despite the showers of rose petals and the adulation.

And watch your back. You are enviable.

Reversed: Passive aggression, false friends, being overlooked.

Are people behaving in passively aggressive ways to you? Ugly gossip and envy abound in this world. Is someone trying to cut you down to a size that won't make them feel small?

COMBUSTION • FIRE • WANDS • CREATIVE SPIRIT • PURPOSE • WORK • ACTION

Could some of your friends be attracted to you mainly for your high position?

Conversely: if you choose to work quietly and privately, do not be surprised or angry when your contributions go unacknowledged.

SYMBOLS:

- **Flaming giraffes:** An homage to surrealist Salvador Dalí
- **Sunflower:** The sun, a glorious crown
- **Rose petals:** Accolades
- **Rose garland crown:** Merit

MINOR ARCANA

COMBUSTION • FIRE • WANDS • CREATIVE SPIRIT • PURPOSE • WORK • ACTION

Seven of Combustion

Seven wig-wearing examiners scrutinize an applicant. She looms large over their little group, holding a small hand mirror turned to face them. The mirror emits thick white smoke, which surrounds the group and obscures the formal edifice in the background.

She is calm and composed, with a wry smile and a direct gaze. She wears a jaunty red hat sporting a gold tassel, has a blue chameleon on her shoulder, and conceals an orange in her left hand.

INTERPRETATION:

Turn the smoke and mirrors back onto those who would mislead you.

Upright: To achieve success, speak up for yourself. This is a good time for courage, self-confidence, and determination. Do not accept clouds of obfuscation from people sitting in judgment against you. Mirror your truth back at them.

If you are in an embattled situation at work, lies may be circulating behind your back. Is there gaslighting or mansplaining?

COMBUSTION • FIRE • WANDS • CREATIVE SPIRIT • PURPOSE • WORK • ACTION

If you are in competition with someone who depends on lies, your success depends upon exposing those lies.

Yet, you have an orange, a little bit of sunshine, in your hand. You have more resources than you realize.

Reversed: If you back down now, you will lose an advantage. Confronting opponents is difficult, but that's your task.

Be your own best friend! Do not permit anyone to bully you, especially with lies. Do not give in to anxiety or self-doubt. If you don't stick up for yourself, who will?

SYMBOLS:

- **Smoke:** Lies and concealed information
- **Mirror:** The ability to reflect unwarranted criticism right back at your detractors
- **Chameleon:** Adaptability
- **Orange:** Extra resources

COMBUSTION • FIRE • WANDS • CREATIVE SPIRIT • PURPOSE • WORK • ACTION

Eight of Combustion

The full moon smiles serenely above a harborside celebration. Elegant buildings flank the water; this is a prosperous city. A festive crowd lines the sea wall. Multicolored fireworks shoot skyward, lighting up the summer night.

INTERPRETATION:

Your endeavors are really taking off! Shoot for the moon!

Upright: Prepare yourself; rapid positive change is on the way.
You can hope for congratulatory messages, unexpected travel, an invitation to a party, a surprising job offer, or good financial news out of the blue.

Or you are experiencing a meteoric rise in your career. Celebrate! Let yourself run with it!

Remember, if you aim for the stars but reach only the moon, that still counts as a victory.

COMBUSTION • FIRE • WANDS • CREATIVE SPIRIT • PURPOSE • WORK • ACTION

Reversed: You can expect unexpected, and potentially unwelcome, news. This news is likely to be destabilizing, challenging, or less than happy.

There may be deep emotional undercurrents swirling around this news, but sometimes the news is merely startling.

Don't let swiftly moving situations unnerve you. Rapid change is difficult for many people. The only practical option is to relax and adapt.

Melting down into emotional fireworks when you are frustrated does not help. Calm yourself and maintain your composure, especially in public.

SYMBOLS:

- **Full moon:** Selene is smiling on a lovely summer's eve
- **Skyrockets:** Sheer joy, celebration, rapid ascension
- **Bonfire:** Big, blazing energy

MINOR ARCANA

COMBUSTION • FIRE • WANDS • CREATIVE SPIRIT • PURPOSE • WORK • ACTION

Nine of Combustion

A man with a stoic expression sits cross-legged on a floating carpet. He is wrapped in a tangerine robe, with his slippers and a large bowl of oranges beside him. He appears unperturbed by the volcano erupting behind him. Sulfurous clouds, rivers of lava, and nine fireballs shoot from the caldera. Disaster threatens everything below the volcano. He understands the danger and accepts his peril.

INTERPRETATION:

Hard work and a will of iron allow you to overcome enormous obstacles. Perseverance, self-discipline, fearlessness.

Upright: You have achieved wisdom and self-discipline through challenging experiences. You will continue to need great inner strength and endurance for the time being. Keep doing what you are doing, and you will live to thrive.

COMBUSTION • FIRE • WANDS • CREATIVE SPIRIT • PURPOSE • WORK • ACTION

Despite the difficulties of life in a cratered moonscape during a volcanic eruption, you have mastered yourself to a fine degree. You are able to face adversity calmly, and to rise above difficult circumstances. By practicing extreme self-reliance, you have now put the worst behind you.

Reversed: Are you experiencing a repeating pattern of failures in some aspect of your life, professional or personal?

Many people respond to suffering by looking outward. They blame other people or bad circumstances for their plight. Yet, feeling victimized has never helped anyone make personal progress.

Try turning within. How do you contribute to your own downfall? Heal self-destructive patterns within you, or you may repeat them.

SYMBOLS:

- **Volcano:** A disaster in the past, power concealed deeply within a mountain
- **Flying carpet:** The ability to rise above challenging circumstances
- **Bowl of oranges:** Plentiful resources at hand

MINOR ARCANA

COMBUSTION • FIRE • WANDS • CREATIVE SPIRIT • PURPOSE • WORK • ACTION

Ten of Combustion

A woman in red, who appears to be both exasperated and overwhelmed, leans back in her chair. She is weighed down by an elaborate metal headdress. It shoots flames from two large openings and supports eight burning candles. The space around her fills with dark smoke.

Evidently, she is not aware of the flying dragon lizard about to land in her lap. But surely she knows about the scaly toes peeking out from under the hem of her dress.

INTERPRETATION:

Now that you are in charge of it all, don't you feel a bit overwhelmed?

Upright: You are experiencing a toxic combination of stress and overload. No matter whether the stress is related to your profession or your personal life, it is imperative that you seek relief now.

The burdens you are managing have affected all aspects of your being. How can you destress enough to regain your serenity? What responsibilities could you delegate to others?

MINOR ARCANA

COMBUSTION • FIRE • WANDS • CREATIVE SPIRIT • PURPOSE • WORK • ACTION

Reversed: You are experiencing relief from crushing responsibilities. Whether the relief comes about because of a joyous or tragic conclusion, finally there is relief. Take time to nourish your body, mind, and spirit. You deserve a break, even some pampering, after what you've been through.

SYMBOLS:

- **Chandelier headgear:** A heavy weight to carry
- **Smoke:** Toxic atmosphere
- **Dragon feet:** An uneasy foundation, underlying chaos, true nature
- **Flying dragon lizard:** *Draco volans,* a mini-dragon perfect for apartment dwellers, a welcome ally

MINOR ARCANA

COMBUSTION • FIRE • WANDS • CREATIVE SPIRIT • PURPOSE • WORK • ACTION

Page of Combustion

A beautiful child, sumptuously dressed in velvet and gold braid, holds the leash of a pet salamander. The child is crowned with a single flame. Circling moths are irresistibly drawn to the bright light.

The floor beneath the page's little pink boots is a checkerboard, suggesting that a game or competition may be about to begin.

INTERPRETATION:

The Page of Combustion ignites the creative spark.

Upright: An energetic and enthusiastic person, a spirit of adventure and discovery. This person enjoys teamwork and energizes everyone else in the group. People are naturally drawn to those who resonate with the brilliant, fiery Page of Combustion.

As a herald, this Page announces surprising revelations or exposes old secrets. This Page enjoys new challenges and embraces forward-thinking social movements or new business developments.

MINOR ARCANA

COMBUSTION • FIRE • WANDS • CREATIVE SPIRIT • PURPOSE • WORK • ACTION

Reversed: Enthusiasm sometimes conceals an unreliable nature.

In reversal, the Page of Combustion can be an irresponsible, immature person. Watch for discrepancies between what they promise and what they deliver. When the Page of Combustion is very poorly aspected, this card speaks to deliberate mischief and pot-stirring.

In terms of a situation, this reversed Page suggests annoying delays, lack of momentum, difficulties maintaining creative flow, scheduling issues.

This card sometimes describes a person with an attention deficit disorder. If upright, they manage well; when reversed, they tend to be organizationally challenged.

SYMBOLS:

- **Moths:** Drawn to the flame
- **Little pink boots:** A sense of whimsy
- **Salamander:** Fire elemental, or a cute little amphibian that lives under damp logs

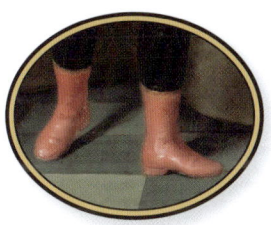

MINOR ARCANA

COMBUSTION • FIRE • WANDS • CREATIVE SPIRIT • PURPOSE • WORK • ACTION

Knight of Combustion

A city is in flames; chaos reigns. A saffron-robed knight contemplates a small green dragon squirming at his feet. He holds back his sword as he decides the creature's fate. Curiously, the dragon is holding a burning match. Could it have started the fire?

The knight's panicked horse rears and squeals. People flee, while an ox roams through the destruction. But despite the distractions, the knight remains focused on the task at hand.

INTERPRETATION:

Although he is a manly man of manly deeds, the Knight of Combustion pauses to weigh the consequences of his actions: Should he spare or slay this scaly beast?

Upright: Here is a passionate person, able to focus and direct power, able to achieve worldly ambition. They are a capable leader working to accomplish their goals. This is someone who has themselves under control, who is dependably responsible and ethical. They have a will of iron, they routinely take a detached point of view, and they take the time to make considered decisions.

COMBUSTION • FIRE • WANDS • CREATIVE SPIRIT • PURPOSE • WORK • ACTION

Passion strongly allied with rational thought. Creativity in business or the arts, responsible behavior leading to good outcomes.

Reversed: When this Knight is reversed, the person or situation this card describes is volatile, explosive, and a loose cannon.

Here, the dragon hovers above the figure of the man. In the heat of the moment, this person acts and reacts without thinking. Their ambition overpowers their ability to listen to reason and can compromise their ethics. Be wary, tread cautiously, lest you spark an overreaction.

SYMBOLS:

- **Dragon:** Chaos, lower self
- **Ox:** Controlled power, self-control
- **Panicked horse:** Unbridled power, destabilizing emotions
- **Burning match:** Why would a dragon need a match?

Boadicea's Tarot of Earthly Delights

MINOR ARCANA

COMBUSTION • FIRE • WANDS • CREATIVE SPIRIT • PURPOSE • WORK • ACTION

Queen of Combustion

Burning torches line a royal chamber. The Queen, seated on a marble bench, takes a rare moment to rest in the midst of her duties. She is dressed in crimson satin and velvet, with a ruby-studded cap on her head. She stares pensively into the middle distance as she thoughtfully taps her fan against the bench. She has decisions to make, orders to give. There is a kingdom—and a king—to be ruled.

Servants bustle about the chamber, her priest wanders by aimlessly, and her pampered black cat notices us watching his mistress.

INTERPRETATION:

The Queen of Combustion is a creative and efficient manager. Under her leadership, her minions accomplish great deeds. There are no idle hours in her realm.

Upright: This queen is knowledgeable, skilled, and charismatic. She is a grande dame, a powerful leader, someone who holds herself to the same high standards she demands from her staff. She is commanding but not cruel.

COMBUSTION • FIRE • WANDS • CREATIVE SPIRIT • PURPOSE • WORK • ACTION

The Queen of Combustion guides when she can, but she is willing to goad her staff if necessary to achieve her goals. She often maintains cordial relationships with her employees after they leave. She enjoys continuing to mentor people she's trained.

But woe betide employees skimping, scamming, or hiding problems from her. Do not tease this tiger! If you do, there will surely be regrets to follow!

Reversed: The reversed Queen of Combustion can be a tone-deaf narcissist, someone who has achieved power for all the wrong reasons. Sometimes she is a schemer, a micromanager, or simply clueless.

At her worst, the reversed Queen enjoys playing cat-and-mouse mind games. Watch your back.

SYMBOLS:
- **A smoke-filled room:** Where real work gets done
- **Numerous minions:** For delegating
- **Personal priest:** Access to spiritual authority
- **Black cat:** Magical companion or familiar, discretion, a watcher
- **Spare crown:** For official appearances

MINOR ARCANA

COMBUSTION • FIRE • WANDS • CREATIVE SPIRIT • PURPOSE • WORK • ACTION

King of Combustion

From his intelligent dark eyes, graying temples, and expressive white hands, it's evident that this king wields his power with judgment and conviction.

Behind him a fantasy rail yard flanks his broad shoulders. His gleaming black top hat spews forth a great cloud of smoke and cinders. It is kept nice and shiny by two puny minions with a rickety ladder. The pattern of workers woven into his coat reminds us that although he may be a captain of industry, they are the ones who actually implement his visions.

INTERPRETATION:

The King of Combustion is charismatic, single-minded, and extremely well organized. As he leads, others follow. Ambitious projects are in the works.

Upright: A forceful and visionary leader. This person is intensely charismatic. They dominate the scene wherever they are. Here is a rainmaker, someone who brings new business to the whole company.

As an executive decision-maker, this person understands how to choose capable department heads, how to guide them effectively, and how to avoid micromanaging.

COMBUSTION • FIRE • WANDS • CREATIVE SPIRIT • PURPOSE • WORK • ACTION

Reversed: People who wield power without compassion often believe that the end justifies the means. That belief is harmful to their characters, and even their souls, besides being objectively false.

Greed and a desire to dominate others are hallmarks of this King in reversal. He asks himself two questions about other people. Are they useful to him? If so, how?

Exploiting people and situations for personal gain, unethical business practices, and unfettered ambition corrode the vessel and degrade our world.

SYMBOLS:

- **Rail yard:** Industry, technological progress, forward thinking
- **Book:** Intelligence, knowledge, study, preparation
- **Bejeweled rings:** Wealth and privilege
- **The little people:** Power behind the throne

TENTACLES • WATER • CUPS • EMOTIONS • INTUITION • RELATIONSHIPS

Ace of Tentacles

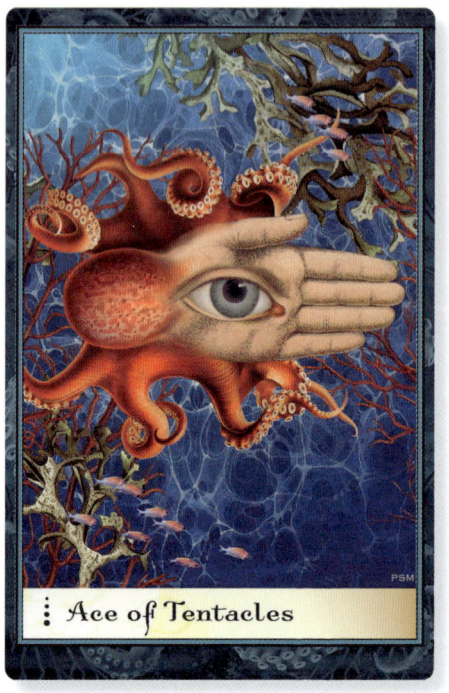

Ace of Tentacles

*The Hamsa Hand of protection manifests in octopodian form.
The eye that sees all and understands all casts an immersive spell from the watery depths. It swims through floating Sargasso weed and bright schools of tiny fish in a sun-dappled sea.*

INTERPRETATION:

Feelings! So many feelings coming your way! Know yourself, know your feelings, and let your feelings flow.

When the Ace of Tentacles appears in a spread, the emotional qualities and motivations affecting the question will be further described in nearby cards.

Upright: How do you *really* feel? Emotions simply are. Be authentic, know yourself.

Dive deeply within and swim with the fishes in the sea of your own emotions. Meditate on your own feelings, seek clarity, and be truthful. Give yourself permission to feel your own emotions, whether or not you can act on them, whether or not your feelings change anything. Being truthful to yourself about your own emotions can improve your mental health.

TENTACLES • WATER • CUPS • EMOTIONS • INTUITION • RELATIONSHIPS

New friends, new love, a new family member, tender feelings, or a honeymoon period in a long-term relationship. Positive emotions, whatever the source.

Reversed: Wait for it! Now is a good time to be cautious and discerning. Are you becoming involved with someone who is wrong for you, someone who might even endanger you?

Or is someone misleading you, preying on your emotions, or gaslighting you? Emotions are fragile. Trust and safe boundaries are very important.

SYMBOLS:

- **Hand:** The ability to influence or manipulate the emotions of others
- **Eye:** Perception, insight into the human psyche
- **Little fishes:** Thoughts and feelings flitting though the heart and mind

TENTACLES • WATER • CUPS • EMOTIONS • INTUITION • RELATIONSHIPS

Two of Tentacles

A male and female clasp hands. His squid and her octopus tentacles entwine suggestively. She engages the viewer with a coquettish smile. His interest is definitely piqued!

These roles are not foreordained by gender. All genders and orientations can play either role. The Two of Tentacles is more likely to be about a sexual or romantic relationship than The Lovers card is.

INTERPRETATION:

This semicephalopodic pair speaks about love, sexual attraction between two people, a deepening emotional relationship, or, sometimes, an unexpected emotional entanglement.

Upright: Come together, right now. A new romantic relationship, or sometimes a deepening friendship of the heart.

Harmony, commitment, engagement leading to marriage, partnering with integrity, or, sometimes, a platonic merging with another person over shared interests or a shared project.

Love is. Emotions are. Sometimes love and attraction are inconvenient, sometimes it is impossible or unethical to act upon our feelings, and sometimes love hurts a lot. We can control our behavior, but we need to feel our feelings nonetheless.

TENTACLES • WATER • CUPS • EMOTIONS • INTUITION • RELATIONSHIPS

Reversed: Keep your tentacles to yourself in public!
   Deception or coercion regarding love and sex. A clandestine love affair, a friendship with secret benefits, an internet flirtation, sexual harassment, or sometimes plain old-fashioned adultery.
   Are you sure this is what you want? In reversal, this card can indicate a troubled relationship fraught with manipulation, lies, or even abuse. Please seek professional help if your love relationship is actually a love/hate relationship.

SYMBOLS:

◆ **Red dress:** Passion
◆ **Tangled tentacles:** Where do my feelings end and the other person's feelings begin?

TENTACLES • WATER • CUPS • EMOTIONS • INTUITION • RELATIONSHIPS

Three of Tentacles

Three narwhals frolic exuberantly in the turquoise surf. Their tusks thrust heavenward to entwine with the arms of a brilliant orange octopus. In one outstretched tentacle, the octopus brandishes a silver teapot and pours out a shower of colorful sea stars.

INTERPRETATION:

It's party time! Celebrate life's victories and anniversaries in delightful company! Whether you are forming compatible new friendships or recalling the good times with lifelong pals, now is a good time to relax and enjoy.

Upright: Feel the love and share the joy! It's time to celebrate! A happy reunion with kindred spirits, celebrating a milestone successfully accomplished, such as a graduation or a new job. Enjoyable group activities, happy relationships, a new and positive change, hurdles overcome in matters of personal or spiritual growth, or meeting new and fascinating friends.

TENTACLES • WATER • CUPS • EMOTIONS • INTUITION • RELATIONSHIPS

Reversed: It's no party, and I'll cry if I need to. There's still a celebration, but not the happiest kind. Isolation, introversion, lack of community.

Learn to savor life's bittersweet moments alongside the sweet ones. In bereavement, the memory of lost love is a testament to its power: the sweetness of love and the pain of loss entwined together.

Don't be shy; let yourself celebrate life's victories and joys when they take place. You may get only one chance to join a Narwhal Tea Party!

When surrounded by negative cards, especially if adjacent to The Devil, this reversal sometimes hints at alcoholism.

SYMBOLS:

- **Silver teapot:** Party ware for a special occasion
- **Star(fish):** Wishes come true
- **Narwhals:** Unicorns of the sea

MINOR ARCANA

TENTACLES • WATER • CUPS • EMOTIONS • INTUITION • RELATIONSHIPS

Four of Tentacles

A stalwart maid stands on stone steps at the edge of a Venetian canal. She holds a foppish white nudibranch by the tail, its head trailing in the water at her feet. Her disdainful expression shows her scorn for the slimy beast.

Three of the sea slug's compatriots float nearby, offering themselves. Behind the maid, there is a lovely garden. Opulent palazzos flank the canal, and a gondola bobs gently in the background.

But she is a servant. She cannot relax and enjoy her lavish surroundings. Her job is to grapple with a sea slug.

INTERPRETATION:

It is important to choose your nudibranchia wisely. Some people are never satisfied. If even the fanciest nudibranch is not good enough for you, it's time to find a new canal.

Upright: Frustration with available options, sometimes narcissism, entitlement, or lack of appreciation.

When you don't like any of the choices available to you, it's time to plan a course correction. What is the next best step you could take to give yourself a better range of choices? Would more training help?

TENTACLES • WATER • CUPS • EMOTIONS • INTUITION • RELATIONSHIPS

No one really wants to be in charge of procuring fancy but venomous sea slugs.

What have you learned from grappling with nudibranchia? How can you apply those lessons to a less toxic, less slimy job?

Reversed: Meh. When your heart isn't in it anymore, it's best to disengage.

Refusal to try anything new when old patterns no longer serve. Disappointment, frustration, intransigence. Clinging to outworn forms of thought and behavior.

It's time to move along now. Permitting anger, resentment, or depression to sideline you will only prolong your pain. Find your core. You are stronger than you realize.

SYMBOLS:

- **Venice:** A city of reflections and water, one of the most beautiful places in the world
- **Palazzos (palaces):** Comfort, plenty, even luxury
- **Gondola:** Means of escape are available
- **Nudibranchia:** Venomous, hermaphroditic, occasionally cannibalistic creatures

TENTACLES • WATER • CUPS • EMOTIONS • INTUITION • RELATIONSHIPS

Five of Tentacles

A small fleet of ships disappear over the horizon, their five masts visible in the bright moonlight. Onshore, a woman looks out to sea and waves farewell. She is wearing a white Renaissance-style gown, enhanced with a pallid tentacle train. Soft waves lap at her feet.

INTERPRETATION:

Disappointment, grief, and loss are painful. It doesn't help to brood over past losses.

Upright: Disappointments and losses are inevitable in life. Don't permit yourself to mourn yesterday's sorrows, while turning your back on today's joys.

How do you respond to challenging emotions? Will you take the time to seethe or grieve, to put your feelings to rest, and then move on emotionally? Will you deny your resentment, sorrow, or rage? Will you drown your misery?

Seek your own inner strength, and you will be better able to weather life's disappointments. Step out of the chancy moonlight into the brighter light of day. Learn to be resilient for the best lifelong results.

TENTACLES • WATER • CUPS • EMOTIONS • INTUITION • RELATIONSHIPS

Reversed: Continuing to mourn long past sorrow is distracting you from life's sunnier days. Don't permit fear of past negative outcomes to hinder progress in the present.

It's time to get your head back into the present, or you risk your future. The ships of the past have sailed! Turn away from the dark waters and go forward with a brave heart.

SYMBOLS:

- **The moon and the sea:** The eternal cycle of the tides
- **Broken reflections of moonlight on water:** Selective memory. We choose and edit how we remember the past.
- **Woman in white facing away:** An enigmatic and mysterious figure
- **Ships in the night:** They pass and leave no trace behind

TENTACLES • WATER • CUPS • EMOTIONS • INTUITION • RELATIONSHIPS

Six of Tentacles

Six children amuse themselves with a game of their own devising. Led by two youths, the younger ones collect flowerlike sea anemones. The children are gathered around a gentle giant squid that lies calmly across the tide pools.

Their cozy homes border the lagoon behind them. This is their favorite playground, and the squid is a cherished pet.

INTERPRETATION:

You may be enjoying peaceful contentment or feeling sweetly nostalgic for simpler, happier times.

Upright: You can go home again. Experience simple pleasures and the security of familiar surroundings.

Contentment, comfort, serenity. In memory, the sun is shining gently, the tide is always just right, the squid relishes the attention, siblings never quarrel, no one gets hurt, and there are plenty of anemones in the garden.

MINOR ARCANA

TENTACLES • WATER • CUPS • EMOTIONS • INTUITION • RELATIONSHIPS

This is a happy period, with few worries or emotional complications. It's a good time to be with family members, kindred spirits, or other dear ones.

Reversed: No, you can't go home again, and it's better not to try. Avoid telling yourself sentimental lies about the past. Make sure nostalgia does not cloud your memories.

Do not delude yourself. Past times were challenging and stressful, as well as pleasant and loving. The past may feel safe now, but only because you know how your past challenges resolved.

Remembering the past accurately is the only way to learn from it.

SYMBOLS:

- **Children:** Innocence, carefree youth
- **Tudor cottages:** Cozy homelife, security, old-fashioned comfort
- **Sea anemones:** Sea flowers, pretty things, simple joys
- **Mr. Squid:** A real or an imaginary friend? Does it matter?
- **Tidal pools:** Ceaseless cycles of change with the flowing tides

MINOR ARCANA

TENTACLES • WATER • CUPS • EMOTIONS • INTUITION • RELATIONSHIPS

Seven of Tentacles

In a watery realm outside her window, a woman analyzes an array of desirable options. Seven tantalizing items representing her possible choices dangle from the arms of an obliging octopus.

On this side of the window, her tabby cat naps on a comfy chair and her companion is reflected in the glass. Despite the room's comforts, the woman may desire more from life. Is she longing for adventures beyond her cozy domestic existence?

INTERPRETATION:

Dreams, aspirations, temptations, desires, distractions: How do you discern among them?

Upright: You've already achieved a lot in your life, but ambition makes you want to reach for more. You are at a pivot point, a time of choice, right now. You have conjured a veritable smörgåsbord of intriguing choices for yourself. What will you choose?

TENTACLES • WATER • CUPS • EMOTIONS • INTUITION • RELATIONSHIPS

Reversed: Are you facing too many choices to make at once? What do you really want? Which potential paths are realistically available to you?

Or are you limited to only a few choices at this time, and none of those choices are to your liking?

Ask yourself what the next step you could take toward happiness and fulfillment might be, and draw another card.

SYMBOLS:

- **Skull and crown:** Mortal, political power
- **Strawberries:** Sensual pleasures
- **Naked youth:** Sexual passion, physical vitality, excellent health
- **Church:** Salvation, ideology, comfort in faith
- **Treasure chest:** Great wealth
- **Teapot and teacup:** Love, to give and receive in a fulfilling partnership or family life
- **Pocket watch:** All the time in the world
- **Spider:** Weaver of dreams
- **Two bottles of liquid:** Love Potion No. 9 and Sugar-Free Love Potion No. 9
- **Napping cat:** Contentment
- **Mouse:** Oh, that little nibbling hint of doubt

Boadicea's Tarot of Earthly Delights

TENTACLES • WATER • CUPS • EMOTIONS • INTUITION • RELATIONSHIPS

Eight of Tentacles

Glancing warily behind him, a man strides away from the eight writhing tentacles reaching out to ensnare him.

In the background, a slender bridge links an obscure island to the shore. The full moon casts dramatic shadows over the watery landscape.

The man is confident and well armed, with two daggers and a sword. He is perfectly capable of dealing with the situation, but he chooses to walk away.

INTERPRETATION:

Sometimes you just have to walk away from The Crazy.

Upright: Consider the possibility of disengaging from your current stressful situation. What would it take for you to walk away and leave The Crazy behind? Are you putting yourself, your needs, and the needs of those who depend on you first? Everyone is more empowered, everyone can make more progress in life, when we do not have to deal with The Crazy.

When The Crazy manifests in a family member or troubled colleague at your workplace, and you literally cannot walk away: it's important to create and enforce safe boundaries for yourself. Carve out some hours

TENTACLES • WATER • CUPS • EMOTIONS • INTUITION • RELATIONSHIPS

each day in which The Crazy is not allowed to disturb you unless there is a dire emergency.

Reversed: You only think you are nailed to your perch. Have you considered all the possibilities?

Are you sure you are out of options? What can you do to prioritize yourself and your own needs in your life?

SYMBOLS:

- **Grasping, tangled tentacles:** The Crazy. The Crazy takes innumerable forms: intrusive or abusive family members, workplace Crazy or Crazy coworker, any Crazy organizational dysfunction
- **Bridge:** A way across difficulties, a higher road to an emotionally safer place
- **Full moon obscured by clouds:** The situation is full of emotion. Clouds hint at possible lies or gaslighting.
- **Moonlight reflected on water:** Long-held emotion deeply considered, or deserving of deep consideration
- **Crescent-shaped hat ornament:** The phases of the moon and a solar eclipse, the mysterious moon obscuring the direct light of sunny reason

TENTACLES • WATER • CUPS • EMOTIONS • INTUITION • RELATIONSHIPS

Nine of Tentacles

Nine colorful sea anemones surround a most contented fellow. He has found his heart's desire: a very handsome cuttlefish. The bard shares his happiness by making beautiful music with his unusual instrument.

INTERPRETATION:

Happy, happy, joy, joy! Wishes that come true.

Upright: Whatever you want. Whatever you really, really want. Contentment and prosperity as a result of long-term hard work. Satisfaction from personal achievement. Generous hospitality: wine, good company, music, good times.

Consider your heart's desire carefully before you send your wish out to the universe. What do you really want? Think before you ask for your heart's desire.

Fairy tales teach us to consider the consequences of our wishes carefully in advance: we can expect those consequences to come rolling back to us.

TENTACLES • WATER • CUPS • EMOTIONS • INTUITION • RELATIONSHIPS

Reversed: Heart's desire-level wishes have serious consequences. Be careful what you wish for in this world. Is your wish wise or foolish, selfish, generous, or somewhere in between?

Or are you dedicating yourself to wine, good company, and music, to the impoverishment of more-practical pursuits? At worst, this card shades into smug self-satisfaction, vulgar displays of wealth, and alcoholism.

SYMBOLS:

- **Red hat:** Indicates a clever individual
- **Cuttlefish:** Neither a lute nor a lutefisk, but a very emotional ocean being: they express their feelings by changing color
- **Clown fish:** Friendship and creative symbiosis: sea anemones and clown fish live in balanced symbiotic harmony

TENTACLES • WATER • CUPS • EMOTIONS • INTUITION • RELATIONSHIPS

Ten of Tentacles

A seaside vision of domestic bliss: two children frolic, a couple walk their dog while enjoying their time together, and an older woman cares for a little one and her pup. Their cozy cottage is crowned with a rainbow that ends where a Kraken is rising from the surf.

INTERPRETATION:

Welcome to happily ever after! Here you are, at the picture-perfect ending of your dreams.

("Kraken? What Kraken? I don't see a Kraken. . .")

Upright: True love, happy families united in harmony, and lifelong domestic contentment to complete the picture.

Treasure times of peace and harmony. Let yourself bask in those fleeting golden moments, now and in memory. Let yourself feel the love, and those happy memories will nourish your heart and soul.

Part of the charm of happy moments is their evanescence. There is always some damned Kraken looming on life's horizon.

TENTACLES • WATER • CUPS • EMOTIONS • INTUITION • RELATIONSHIPS

Reversed: Is this your dream, or your nightmare? Does domestic bliss make you want to flee? While domestic bliss is not for everyone, it is worth examining the roots of this aversion in a quest for self-understanding.

Or do you crave a wider group of friends, or a committed relationship, but find such relationships elusive? Are you doing anything practical to manifest the relationships you seek? There are kindred spirits everywhere. To meet people, you must reach out.

SYMBOLS:

- **Rainbow:** Hope's promise
- **Rose-covered cottage by the sea:** Happy ever after
- **Children playing:** Carefree, joyous optimism
- **Mature adults:** A life well lived, caring for others, multigenerational ties
- **Dogs:** Unconditional love, emotional fidelity
- **The Kraken:** Dammit, there's always something coming down the pike . . .

TENTACLES • WATER • CUPS • EMOTIONS • INTUITION • RELATIONSHIPS

Page of Tentacles

A dark-haired young woman in a simple white dress dances along the edge of a massive waterfall. She is cloaked in two ornate nudibranchia, and she brandishes a spotted eel.

A puzzled fish inquiringly peers up from the edge of the falls. The mists rising from the torrent are brightened by a double rainbow.

INTERPRETATION:

The Page of Tentacles brings tidings of emotional or romantic matters, along with an eel.

Upright: A naive person, or someone temperamentally innocent. Younger family members, teens, or children. A young or inexperienced person who finds themselves in deep emotional waters. Emotional risk-taking with a positive outcome.

Good news of a wedding, an announcement about a new relationship, a person coming out to their community about their true nature, or other news of an emotional milestone.

TENTACLES • WATER • CUPS • EMOTIONS • INTUITION • RELATIONSHIPS

Too inexperienced to be afraid of dancing at the edge of a waterfall, this Page skillfully navigates the precipice, while twirling her eel with joyous abandon. Her accomplishment is noteworthy, even unique, as the surprised fish attests.

Reversed: A callow youth churning with chaotic emotions. Someone whose immaturity causes problems in relationships, whether romantic or otherwise.

A young person suffering from the effects of emotional abuse. An emotional breakdown, such as manifesting obsessive-compulsive behavior, or an eating disorder. If The Devil is nearby, this reversal hints at a drinking problem.

SYMBOLS:

- **Waterfall:** Dynamic, fluid energy
- **White dress:** Innocence, pure heart
- **Nudibranchia:** Feelings, so many complicated feelings
- **Eel:** Slippery and difficult to handle
- **That perturbed fish:** Something surprising, an emotional wild card

TENTACLES • WATER • CUPS • EMOTIONS • INTUITION • RELATIONSHIPS

Knight of Tentacles

Waves pound against a rocky cliff. A rider gallops his horse through the tide pools, disturbing creatures below. He wears a spiffy uniform, and indescribably tentacled headgear. He brandishes a big, red, swordlike squid. The rider is not minding where he is going, but fortunately, the horse is paying attention.

The impetuous Knight of Tentacles is a catalyst, setting the interpersonal relationships around him spinning. He is enthusiastic and outspoken, but not very tactful.

Knight of Tentacles

INTERPRETATION:

Here is a young person willing, even eager, to risk any amount of sorrow in their search for joy.

Upright: The Knight of Tentacles embodies an impulsive yet endearing young person, a person who is very sweet and loads of fun, but not very reliable.

Be warned. The Knight is risking his horse in slippery tidal pools, and his horse is crushing living shellfish beneath his hooves. The Knight's focused emotions blind him to his own insensitivity.

Or he could be heralding an exciting and fast-moving romantic affair.

TENTACLES • WATER • CUPS • EMOTIONS • INTUITION • RELATIONSHIPS

Reversed: This reversed Knight has lost control of his emotions completely.

An unfaithful lover, a gossipy troublemaker, or a shameless flirt. At worst, a stalker.

Be careful with your heart. It's only wise to maintain strong personal boundaries around such people like these.

Or is this you? Do you need to filter yourself more carefully? If you can stand home truths, ask a close friend their frank opinion of your communication skills.

SYMBOLS:

- **Charging horse:** Impetuous activity
- **Ocean waves:** Dynamic, fluid energy
- **Crashing surf:** Emotional conflict
- **Trampled shellfish:** No respect for boundaries, careless of causing harm to others
- **A wiggly squid:** Strong impulses that may be hard to handle
- **Spiny lobster:** Consciousness emerging out of obscurity

MINOR ARCANA

TENTACLES • WATER • CUPS • EMOTIONS • INTUITION • RELATIONSHIPS

Queen of Tentacles

Like an Aphrodite of the Cephalopods, the Queen of Tentacles rises from the deep. Her voluptuous form is enhanced by golden tentacles as well as four lovely human arms. She floats effortlessly, framed by red sea fans and tropical fishes. She wears a coral crown adorned with a single scarlet sea star. Her chestnut hair waves in the water. Around her the blue-black sea is spangled with bioluminescent stars.

INTERPRETATION:

The Queen of Tentacles is a passionate, desirable, sensual, and loving being.

Upright: A wise and emotionally warm individual. A lover or spouse who makes you feel loved and brings you great joy. The power of love, whether spiritual, familial, or physical. The knowledge that you are deeply loved. Sensual bodily pleasure. The beloved. The best sex. When expressed platonically, a loving spiritual leader, a close friend.

Knowing that we are deeply loved supports our ability to love others. Being loved, especially being well loved in childhood, makes us emotionally sturdier and more resilient to life's challenges.

MINOR ARCANA

TENTACLES • WATER • CUPS • EMOTIONS • INTUITION • RELATIONSHIPS

Reversed: Emotional cruelty. The absence of true affection. Love or passion gone, or gone awry.

Someone who manipulates others by giving or withholding affection. A cold, controlling mother figure, someone jealous, intrusive, and constantly demanding her children's attention.

Unwanted physical attention, boundary violations, being groped. Sex without consent, manipulative sex, sexual dysfunction, unloving sex. When this card is very badly aspected, sexual perversion, even sexual violence.

SYMBOLS:

- **A naked queen:** Pride and confidence in one's own beauty, appreciation of physical affection, bold acknowledgment of desire, flaunting sexual desirability
- **A dark sea spangled with bioluminescent stars:** Deep feelings illuminated with magical points of light
- **Red sea fans:** Pathways and connections
- **Blue-cheeked butterfly fish:** Long-lasting love. This species forms long-term mated pairs, which is rather uncommon in fish.

TENTACLES • WATER • CUPS • EMOTIONS • INTUITION • RELATIONSHIPS

King of Tentacles

This magnificent ruler exudes masculine power and sensuality. He is seated on a classical throne, encrusted by a coral reef. His dark hair and beard sprout gently waving octopus arms. He holds his scepter upright in his right hand and comfortably rests his left on some frilly fan worms.

A reverse mermaid kneels at his feet, clutching his knee. She may be either a lover or a supplicant.

INTERPRETATION:

The King of Tentacles rules from the heart. He is both passionate and compassionate, but sometimes quick to anger.

Upright: Here's an emotionally honest person with an open heart, someone who is reliably kind to others, a loving and responsible partner, a good parent, or a valuable mentor. Compassionate application of justice. Self-control. This person has strong emotional boundaries around deep undercurrents of feeling.

MINOR ARCANA

TENTACLES • WATER • CUPS • EMOTIONS • INTUITION • RELATIONSHIPS

A powerful yet benevolent character, this person feels his emotions deeply but is never ruled by them. He is emotionally true to himself despite his leadership role in life, a relatively rare combination.

Reversed: Power without compassion, emotional domination without responsibility.

This is an emotional tyrant, eager to control other people, someone both petty and cruel. This person has no ability to regulate their emotions, someone who easily devolves into gaslighting or even abusive rage to enforce their will.

A destructive emotional relationship with an authority figure or family member. A parent, stepparent, sibling, or spouse who advances their personal agenda by manipulating others.

SYMBOLS:

- **Coral reef:** The King's flourishing domain is a product of biological cooperation. Coral, a symbiotic life form of a polyp and an algae, together build massive reef structures that support myriad creatures.
- **Jellyfish-crowned scepter:** Those who wield great power may dole out either great blessings or painful stings.
- **Fishy femme:** Reverse mermaid, a curiously rare mixture of characteristics

Boadicea's Tarot of Earthly Delights

MINOR ARCANA

ÆTHER • AIR • SWORDS • INTELLECT • IDEAS • LOGIC • WIT • DISCOURSE

Ace of Æther

A leather-gloved hand with a wolfish grin flies high above the land. It has beautiful, iridescent wings that sparkle in the rarefied air. It skims over rolling farmland and misty mountains. Eagles glide in the sky above, flying at an even greater altitude than the Ace.

INTERPRETATION:

The Ace of Æther heralds an emerging paradigm. Embrace bold new ideas, and you shall flourish. Deny the obvious, and you may get bitten.

Upright: New approach, novel perspective, and fresh ideas. A mental awakening, inspiration, sudden breakthrough. Startling insight about oneself, other people, or a situation. Perceiving patterns that were previously obscured, by taking a wider view. The ability to rise above challenging circumstances and base instincts to higher ethical and intellectual planes beyond hate and fear.

Communications of all sorts. Power and influence obtained through sophisticated communication skills.

Even at its zenith, the Ace of Æther has sharp teeth and a hard bite.

ÆTHER • AIR • SWORDS • INTELLECT • IDEAS • LOGIC • WIT • DISCOURSE

Reversed: Oh no! Not another blasted epiphany!
On the inside: denial, obfuscation, or refusal to adapt despite changed circumstances. Ennui and stagnation. Lack of imagination or insight.
On the outside: closed minds, unpleasant gossip, deliberate lies. Manipulation of public opinion. Pettiness and pettifoggery. Devotion to form over function, and a focus on minutia. At its nadir, exploitation and criminality.
The most damaging lies are the ones we tell ourselves.

SYMBOLS:

- **Wing(s):** The flight of ideas
- **Flying hand:** All you need is (g)love
- **Glove:** Conscious control, pure ego contained
- **Teeth:** Biting wit
- **Deep-blue sky:** The stratosphere, up where the air is clear
- **Eagles:** Aspirations, lofty ideals, free thinkers, the power of ideas
- **Clouds and mist:** Obfuscation, clouds to reason
- **Mountains:** The wild unknown
- **Farmland:** Common sense, established principles, traditional thought

MINOR ARCANA

ÆTHER • AIR • SWORDS • INTELLECT • IDEAS • LOGIC • WIT • DISCOURSE

Two of Æther

A blindfolded angel kneels on an icy rock. Every feather in her upraised wings is a sharpened blade. These wings of steel and her pearlescent dress reflect the waning winter sun. An owl perches on a bare branch over her right shoulder. In the background a single light shows amid a hamlet of darkened cottages. Storm clouds race across the sky.

She dangles a curious yo-yo decorated with the crescent moon. How does it inform the decision at hand?

Two of Æther

INTERPRETATION:

Time to make up your mind.

Upright: Decisions, decisions. Analyzing the available choices and weighing every aspect before deciding on anything is good practice, even if you are blindfolded, underdressed, and out in the cold. Yet, cycling between contradictions without making a decision eventually stalls all progress.
The owl is hooting a warning: it's time to end the yo-yoing!

ÆTHER • AIR • SWORDS • INTELLECT • IDEAS • LOGIC • WIT • DISCOURSE

What steps could you take toward self-respect and personal fulfillment? What might happen if you simply rip off the blindfold, take wing, and fly away?

Reversed: Refusing to make a choice is a choice in itself. Postponing a difficult decision will not make it any easier.

Some decisions demand self-sacrifice to uphold self-respect. It is easy to turn away from making hard decisions requiring self-sacrifice: self-sacrifice is inherently uncomfortable. However, self-love hinges on self-respect. Until people face their fears and look deeply within, they cannot take wing and fly.

SYMBOLS:

- **Blindfolded figure:** Inner reason over outward appearances
- **Wings of steel:** Occam's razor
- **Winter:** A cold season calls for cold reason, a good time for reflection,
  and for making plans for the future
- **White owl:** Pure wisdom, rational mind
- **A single lighted window:** If the lights are on, somebody's home, indicating ongoing, but not necessarily obvious, thought processes
- **Moon yo-yo:** A perpetually shifting balance between logic and reason, emotion and intuition

MINOR ARCANA

ÆTHER • AIR • SWORDS • INTELLECT • IDEAS • LOGIC • WIT • DISCOURSE

Three of Æther

Three beetles tear apart an airborne heart fashioned from a lovely rose bouquet. As the beetles tear at the blossoms, they sully its beauty and ruin its symmetry. Despite this trauma, the heart emits illuminated rays against the dawn sky.

All is not lost! Help is on the way. A flock of swallows, hungry for tasty bugs, are flying in from the South.

INTERPRETATION:

Broken hearts and dashed dreams are deeply painful, but not insurmountable.

Upright: Heartbreak, disillusion, discord. Pointless arguments that go around and around without resolution.

Taking apart a heart full of roses is risky. Will it fit back together again, once the insects have been removed? However, taking apart the heart may be the only way to get rid of the bugs. Kindness, love, and beauty inevitably attract predators. Discernment and strength of character are
our best tools to avoid becoming prey.

130 *Boadicea's Tarot of Earthly Delights*

ÆTHER • AIR • SWORDS • INTELLECT • IDEAS • LOGIC • WIT • DISCOURSE

Reversed: The beginning of the end of heartbreak. Brave heart now.

Roses deserve better than to become a feast for predators. It's time to let go and move on. No satisfactory resolution is available here. Time to leave intractable problems behind.

Sometimes we need to take our hearts and fly away, if we really need to get rid of the bugs.

Your heart is made of roses. Trust that there will be a brighter tomorrow.

SYMBOLS:
- **Rose heart:** Hopes and dreams, love, happiness
- **Beetles:** Destruction, frustration, sorrow and woe
- **Illuminated rays:** The power to heal that comes from within
- **Swallows:** Hope; rescue is on its way.

ÆTHER • AIR • SWORDS • INTELLECT • IDEAS • LOGIC • WIT • DISCOURSE

Four of Æther

Four gray-feathered angel wings embrace a white dove. They hover over a young man napping on a Roman chaise.

The laurel wreath he wears, as well as those decorating his bed, shows his achievements. He sleeps peacefully now, although the rumpled sheets suggest he had been restless. One arm trails across a lyre, a book, and an opium pipe; a sheathed sword hangs from the headboard.

It is sunset, the sky is golden, and the hills below bloom with scarlet poppies. The dove holds a spray of the same flowers. All is well, for this one tranquil moment.

INTERPRETATION:

Forget your worldly cares. You need to rest. It is time for a nice long nap.

Upright: It's time for rest now. Take a temporary retreat from conflict, so you can recover and fight again. Strategic withdrawal. Respite from care. After completing important tasks, it's important to take a break and recover.

ÆTHER • AIR • SWORDS • INTELLECT • IDEAS • LOGIC • WIT • DISCOURSE

Conflict takes a toll on minds as well as bodies. Seek inner peace after a long and stressful time period. This is a warning. It's rest time.

Reversed: Instead of a warning, in reversal, this card is an alarm. It's vital to take time away from responsibilities as soon as possible. People who drive themselves mercilessly tend to sideline themselves by becoming unwell. Do not permit ambition to result in illness, whether it's bodily illness, depression, or alienation. No one gets ahead long term through endless overwork. Endless overwork results in collapse. During the immediately forthcoming rest period, best practice demands an analysis of habitual behavior patterns that support overwork and minimize self-care.

SYMBOLS:

- **Poppies, opium pipe:** Respite from care, oblivion
- **White dove:** Peace
- **Book and lyre:** Intellect at rest
- **Sheathed sword:** An end to conflict
- **Laurels:** Success requiring great effort to achieve

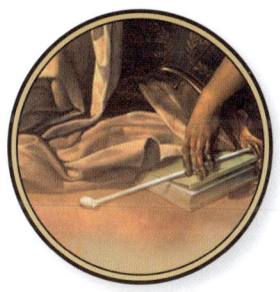

ÆTHER • AIR • SWORDS • INTELLECT • IDEAS • LOGIC • WIT • DISCOURSE

Five of Æther

Chaos reigns. Despite the lightning strikes and crazy, tilted landscape, a resourceful hunter sends his golden eagle in search of prey. Four more birds pierce the clouds above.

He is mature and powerfully built, wearing beautifully woven and embroidered clothing, carrying ingeniously crafted hunting tools. Man and eagle stand on a precipice above a heaving chasm. The world may be turned upside down, but the hunter is unfazed. He has an invaluable partner, the eagle, neither a captive nor a pet.

INTERPRETATION:

Ingenuity is a lifesaver. Willingness to adapt to changing, challenging circumstances can determine our survival, our path to thrive, our eventual triumph.

Upright: Thoughtful problem-solving and careful discernment are necessary during times of rapid change. Adjusting to adversity is challenging, yet necessary to survive. Even in the midst of chaos, it is possible to keep a clear head. Changing circumstances offer opportunities as well as exposing dangerous rifts.

MINOR ARCANA

ÆTHER • AIR • SWORDS • INTELLECT • IDEAS • LOGIC • WIT • DISCOURSE

Change is inevitable. Embracing change promotes innovation and prefigures success, even triumph. This situation requires the mental discipline to walk a knife's-edge path with a deep abyss on either side. Rise like the eagle, take a long-term view, and fly steadily toward the best possible future.

Reversed: It is easy to become overwhelmed in times of rapid change, but falling into inner chaos will not help. Complex situations can be intimidating. It helps to break down tasks into smaller, more manageable increments. It's time to find the inner strength to face unhappy consequences with courage and determination.

SYMBOLS:

- **Chasm:** Unpredictability, obstacles
- **Chaos:** The opposite of order and reason
- **Eagle tamer:** Wild power channeled by will, leadership, ability to take a longer, wider perspective
- **Eagles:** The power of ideas, freedom of thought, freedom of speech, freedom of conscience. Freedom persisting by eternal vigilance.
- **Ruined castles:** Apparent disaster, tearing down the status quo
- **Lightning:** Intense, unpredictable energy, creativity, ideas striking "out of the blue"

MINOR ARCANA

ÆTHER • AIR • SWORDS • INTELLECT • IDEAS • LOGIC • WIT • DISCOURSE

Six of Æther

A winged rowboat piloted by a blind oracle dressed in red flies over the rainbow. The back of the boat is in shadow, and the front is bathed in gentle light.

The young woman seated in the boat wears a frilly white dress and a beribboned hat. She stares ahead dreamily as the oracle rows. The ingenue is shielded from the rising mist by a gold-and-paisley travel rug. Her little pug dog perches on the plank before her, next to a heap of iris that she has gathered along the way.

The boat is held aloft by half a dozen butterfly wings extending from the hull. They are passing over a meandering stream into green fields, leaving behind the ruins of a classical fort.

INTERPRETATION:

You are leaving rainstorms and ruins behind, and flying past the rainbow into sunlight. It's time to move above and beyond, mentally or literally. Take the high road, and your little dog too.

Upright: Put your intuition in charge and rise above the hurly-burly of life. How can you move toward tranquility? Habitually taking a longer perspective in life usually diminishes regrets we may have in retrospect. Leave those ruins behind and follow your own stream of

ÆTHER • AIR • SWORDS • INTELLECT • IDEAS • LOGIC • WIT • DISCOURSE

consciousness beyond the rainbow. There you will know yourself and find inner peace.

Reversed: Beware bad timing. Are you missing the boat by refusing to examine your inner pain? Are you deliberately looking away from festering problems? Remaining silent about problems rarely leads to solutions. Ignoring challenging issues generally prolongs any difficulties. Analyzing your situation can help you break illogical but habitual thought patterns, societal programming, and familial expectations.

Who are you really? What do you think and how do you feel about the ruins and the rainstorm?

SYMBOLS:

- **Rowboat:** Vessel, the body that houses the soul
- **Rainbow:** The rainbow bridge, crossing over
- **Blind oracle:** Fate
- **Ruins:** The past, sorrow or strife
- **River or stream:** Time flowing on
- **Green fields:** A brighter future
- **Iris:** Fleur-de-lis, faith, hope, wisdom and valor
- **Pug dog:** You are not alone; a companion or a dependent (or both)

ÆTHER • AIR • SWORDS • INTELLECT • IDEAS • LOGIC • WIT • DISCOURSE

Seven of Æther

A sly, grinning woman walks away from a lively circus. She grasps a sword sprouting into a laurel branch, with butterflies, a caterpillar, and a large moth perched on it. Her expression suggests that she is up to something, or that she has just gotten away with an act of mischief.

The sky is blue with bright golden clouds, although dark ones peek over the horizon. Chestnut leaves spread across the foreground. They are beginning to turn brown at summer's end.

INTERPRETATION:

Are things really what they seem? Are you being conned, or are you the deceiver?

Upright: Some people feel compelled to grab all the butterflies for themselves, whether by peaceful or criminal means.

If you are being deceived, here is a warning. Who might be lying to you, and why? Start by considering people with financial motives.

Do not permit yourself to lie, to cheat, or to cut corners now. Do not twist truth to suit an ideology or represent yourself in diverse ways before different audiences. These are short-term actions that lead

ÆTHER • AIR • SWORDS • INTELLECT • IDEAS • LOGIC • WIT • DISCOURSE

to longterm troubles. Trust is earned, and honor upheld, through consistently principled behavior.

Reversed: Your suspicions are well founded. Gullible people are being manipulated. But who is the deceiver? To what end are they manipulating people? Could this situation involve conspiracy theories, theft of ideas, or misleading propaganda, comprising a veneer of truth over lies designed to make money?

Examine your own assumptions and beliefs with a critical eye. It's time to investigate. Start with yourself.

SYMBOLS:

- **Sword:** A weapon that cuts both ways
- **Laurel branch:** Peace, honors, and achievement
- **Butterflies, caterpillars, and moths:** Changeable appearances, outer form vs. inner truth
- **Chestnut tree:** Truth and justice—in abundance if nurtured with care, yet susceptible to blight
- **Red hat:** Clever girl
- **Circus:** An entertainment and a distraction; "The show must go on."
- **Elephant:** Who never forgets?

MINOR ARCANA

ÆTHER • AIR • SWORDS • INTELLECT • IDEAS • LOGIC • WIT • DISCOURSE

Eight of Æther

Eight assorted bats careen around the head of a distraught young lady. She has conjured up a birdcage to protect her head. Is the cage keeping the bats out, or containing—and thus constraining—her?

From the neck down, she possesses the body of a gray parrot with a bright-red tail. Dainty human hands sprout from her wing joints. They clutch at her feathered chest in dismay. A dark, forbidding mountain rises behind her. The sea lashes at its base. The sky is lit by a strange, but spectacular, Aurora Borealis.

INTERPRETATION:

Is it all in your head?

Upright: Do not panic! When you are in danger, it is natural to be afraid. However, spiraling into terror won't help you find a way to safety. Calmly examine the reasons for your fears and take courage. Where is the boundary between baseless anxiety and actual danger?

Only you can set yourself free. You have more in common with those bats than you now realize. Try talking to them. If you don't like them once you are out of your cage, you can fly away.

ÆTHER • AIR • SWORDS • INTELLECT • IDEAS • LOGIC • WIT • DISCOURSE

Reversed: Why are you deceiving yourself? It's time to get beyond soothing lies designed to distract you from guilt, shame, fear, and anger. Tell yourself the whole bitter truth. As humans, we are not always able to be on our best behavior. Releasing ourselves from the lies we tell ourselves, forgiving ourselves, and moving on from mistakes are crucial steps toward self-respect and self-reliance.

SYMBOLS:

- **Bats:** Often-misunderstood creatures, occult senses, clairvoyance, night spirits
- **Ethereal cage:** An imagined prison, self-imposed limitations
- **Parrot:** Although African grey parrots are renowned for their intelligence, in this card image the parrot represents repetition without comprehension.
- **Dark mountain:** Could be just a mountain, could be Mount Doom
- **Aurora Borealis:** Unearthly light, evidence of the earth's protective magnetic shield

ÆTHER • AIR • SWORDS • INTELLECT • IDEAS • LOGIC • WIT • DISCOURSE

Nine of Æther

A red velvet curtain has been pulled aside to reveal flying insects trapped in spiderwebs. From her couch below, a nearly naked nymph graced with luna moth wings sprouting behind her ears gestures toward the bug-covered wall.

She appears to be in a trance or fugue state, as she turns dreamy eyes heavenward. Is she ignoring the black widow spider tiptoeing up her leg? Another unsettling item is the jaundiced hand reaching toward her, proffering another moth for the collection.

INTERPRETATION:

Nightmarish anxiety or actual danger? Can you spot the difference?

Upright: Unless you wish to share the fate of the seven moths trapped in the web, take a deep breath, focus, and deal with the venomous spider now. Dwelling on past cruelties and losses is distracting you from imminent dangers.

ÆTHER • AIR • SWORDS • INTELLECT • IDEAS • LOGIC • WIT • DISCOURSE

Do your own thoughts disturb you sometimes? All of us have shadowy, negative aspects to our characters. Integrating your shadow, holding your shadow gently with love under self-discipline, will increase your personal power by a thousandfold. Join with your shadow, accept your power, accept your authentic self.

Reversed: Sorrow, fear, and anger are part of the human condition. Wallowing in cynicism or rage, keeping grief fresh with morbid thoughts, and dwelling in resentment about what life has not given you are forms of self-indulgence. Discipline yourself, deal with your inner turmoil, and you will find peace and serenity.

If you cannot sleep, ask yourself why might that be?

SYMBOLS:
- **Lifted curtain:** Our dark thoughts and shadow selves revealed
- **Spiderwebs:** A gossamer snare
- **Trapped insects:** Imprisoned by their own struggles
- **Black widow spider:** Phobias, nightmares
- **Disembodied hand:** A rather unsettling thing
- **Luna moth:** Alluding to the moon, and its power to reveal what is hidden by the night

MINOR ARCANA

ÆTHER • AIR • SWORDS • INTELLECT • IDEAS • LOGIC • WIT • DISCOURSE

Ten of Æther

One winged tiger—a species of gryphon—faces off nine hungry vultures that are about to devour the remains of a hapless traveler. The protective gryphon wraps a huge paw around the man's bloody chest as the vultures assemble at his feet. The scene unfolds in an unearthly realm, suspended by storm clouds and surrounded by jagged ice walls. Lightning flashes as the vultures squabble.

INTERPRETATION:

When it's too late to change your plans, time to power on through.

Upright: Do not linger in defeat. In difficult circumstances, resolving our challenges as best we can and then moving away rapidly is sometimes the best outcome possible. Try to make a clean break.

Lightning is dangerous and can kill you, but lightning also brings inspiration. New ideas attract detractors as well as allies. When the crowd turns against you, it's the end. However, one magical Tiger-Gryphon is more powerful than nine hungry vultures, and lightning does indeed strike multiple times. Tomorrow is another day.

ÆTHER • AIR • SWORDS • INTELLECT • IDEAS • LOGIC • WIT • DISCOURSE

Reversed: Prolonged messy squabbling over divorce, endless negotiations over estates, bad faith in business matters. Check and double-check any sensitive financial information or contracts; ask for supporting evidence of any allegations that might be questionable. When reversed, the Ten of Æther foretells the end, and an unpleasantly messy one too. Sometimes all we can do is get beyond a bad situation as expeditiously as possible.

SYMBOLS:

- **Winged tiger:** A form of gryphon, guardian of the Divine, symbol of great courage, a powerful psychopomp for the most dire passages
- **Vultures:** Indispensable processors of mortal remains
- **Lightning bolt:** A great surge of sudden power, fatal devastation, divine inspiration, or sudden transformation
- **The scene:** Death and dismemberment by vultures, mediated by a helpful Tiger-Gryphon

MINOR ARCANA

ÆTHER • AIR • SWORDS • INTELLECT • IDEAS • LOGIC • WIT • DISCOURSE

Page of Æther

A free-spirited young woman, clad in a diaphanous wrap, pedals her celestial velocipede across a cloud bank. She gaily flings her arms above her head, trailing colored streamers and dramatically waving a caged owl. Is the owl enjoying itself as much as the gal? A firefly headlamp illuminates her path as she glides on wheels with grasshopper wings as spokes.

INTERPRETATION:

The Page of Æther is an airborne messenger with news to impart or exciting gossip to share. She may bring insight to a developing situation.

    Upright: New ideas, breaking news. Suddenly discovering fresh and surprising information about a past situation. A burst of information and an inclination to experiment. A charming, vivacious person, full of ideas and enthusiasm. This person is more of a cheerleader of wisdom than a wise person in their own right, as their caged owl suggests. A person working in media or advertising, or a brilliant salesperson. A fast talker, someone who makes a wonderful first impression but cannot always sustain respect.

ÆTHER • AIR • SWORDS • INTELLECT • IDEAS • LOGIC • WIT • DISCOURSE

Reversed: A naive person lacking in discretion. A tattletale or a malicious gossip. Fake news, biased reporting of the facts, unreliable information. Style over function, artfully packaged half-truths, partisan infotainment masquerading as news.

A nervous talker, someone who wears out their welcome with constant chatter. A person who is unable to ground themselves in reality. Someone who becomes hysterical when asked to cope. At best, a naive person lacking in discretion. At worst, a tattletale, a malicious gossip, a two-faced backstabber.

SYMBOLS:

- **Velocipede:** Bicycle, speed, momentum
- **Firefly:** A bright idea
- **Streamers:** Freedom, fun, joy
- **Caged owl:** Wisdom constrained, yet to be released

ÆTHER • AIR • SWORDS • INTELLECT • IDEAS • LOGIC • WIT • DISCOURSE

Knight of Æther

Not coincidentally, this knight bears a striking resemblance to Pallas Athena. She throws us a confident glance before spurring her mount into the whirling eye of a hurricane. She is armored in gold and crimson, sits astride a gray stallion on a leopard skin saddle, and carries a wicked long saber. Her great bat wings unfurl in preparation for a righteous battle.

INTERPRETATION:

The Knight of Æther is off to battle the maelstrom, armed with logic, wit, reason, and a pointy, pointy sword.

Upright: Are you confused by polarized, opposing views? Hold steadily to your core beliefs amid the cacophony. Keep listening for your own inner voice until you know your own mind. Stepping back from the maelstrom may help you gain perspective.

The Knight of Æther aggressively defends her ideas and ideals. Whether she is aligned with mercy or severity, she is brilliantly incisive and powerfully effective.

ÆTHER • AIR • SWORDS • INTELLECT • IDEAS • LOGIC • WIT • DISCOURSE

If you are suspicious about some kind of rule-breaking or financial misbehavior, this card suggests that your suspicions are not unfounded.

Reversed: Seeing the world in black and white, by the book, has its risks. Among those risks are intolerance, blind partisanship, and even hard-core zealotry. Who is doing something they know is morally or ethically wrong? Intellectually passive people do not necessarily stick up for what they hold dear, especially when they are opposed by stronger personalities.

To thine own self be true.

SYMBOLS:

◆ **Hurricane:** Chaos, destructive spiral
◆ **Pallas Athena:** Greek goddess of wisdom, handicraft, skill, and warfare
◆ **Sword:** Heroic blade of Truth
◆ **Leopard skin:** Symbol of aristocratic status

ÆTHER • AIR • SWORDS • INTELLECT • IDEAS • LOGIC • WIT • DISCOURSE

Queen of Æther

A smiling Queen stands perfectly balanced on a high branch. The sun has just risen in a tangerine sky. A flock of cobalt butterflies streams toward her lips. She wears opulent gold jewelry and a ruby-studded crown.

Her appearance is both puzzling and amazing: above the waist, she is a joyous winged Harpy. Her feathers are soft and ivory colored; her shoulders and face are beautiful. Below the waist she assumes the classic form of the Venus de Milo. Can an airborne being have marble legs and still fly?

INTERPRETATION:

Witty and vivacious, the Queen of Æther inspires the free flow of ideas. She shapes the discourse around her with insight and diplomacy.

Upright: An open and positive exchange of ideas. Respect for the opinions of others, mutual trust, and fair play. Consensus decision-making. Negotiation instead of bullying. Setting a good example.

An intellectually perceptive individual gifted with foresight and wisdom. A lawyer, or the rainmaker in a business, this charismatic woman easily attracts others to her causes. Fully grounded in hard reality,

ÆTHER • AIR • SWORDS • INTELLECT • IDEAS • LOGIC • WIT • DISCOURSE

this Queen chooses persuasion over force, and mercy over severity, as her superpowers. When setbacks come, this Queen accepts them with grace. She always chooses the high road.

Reversed: Intolerance toward conflicting viewpoints, resistance to honest debate. Zealotry, highly partisan ideological influences, conspiracy theories, disinformation.

An instigator of discord, a mischief-maker who enjoys inciting quarrels. A flim-flam artist who has a twisted relationship with truth. It is not in your self-interest to trust this person. If there is a legal issue, follow the money.

SYMBOLS:

- **Treetop:** A high vantage point, perspective
- **Orange sky:** Dawn(ing)
- **Flock of azure butterflies:** Beautiful words and ideas
- **Feathered wings:** The power of flight, a mercurial mind
- **Marble limbs:** A firm grounding in classical learning, sometimes feet of clay, occasionally both

ÆTHER • AIR • SWORDS • INTELLECT • IDEAS • LOGIC • WIT • DISCOURSE

King of Æther

As with his Queen, this King is a combination of forms. He has the head of a magpie, with a bird's keen eyesight and sharp beak. His body is that of a well-built man. He wears an intricately fashioned crown, a regal ermine cape, and a sky-blue tunic richly decorated with golden thread. His left hand rests on an open book; his right firmly clasps a royal scepter that is crowned by a bejeweled housefly. Two funnel clouds are forming in the sky above his head. Although he is clearly looking forward, he is still well aware of the storm that is brewing behind his back.

King of Æther

INTERPRETATION:

The King of Æther is a sharp-witted and perceptive monarch. He is quick to analyze a situation and swift to pass judgment.

Upright: Magpies belong to the *Corvidae*, a cosmopolitan family of birds known for their intelligence. Leadership based on intellect. Clear thinking and good judgment. A commitment to fair play and justice. A razor-sharp balance between severity and mercy. A visionary leader, someone who can change the world for the better, heralding a good future.

MINOR ARCANA

ÆTHER • AIR • SWORDS • INTELLECT • IDEAS • LOGIC • WIT • DISCOURSE

Decision-making based on science; laws and policies that balance community and individual. A charismatic person who combats the forces of chaos and upholds rectitude and honor. A leader gifted with inspirational ideas, combined with inspirational powers of persuasion.

Reversed: A powerful person lacking insight or good judgment. A bully who greets disagreements with threats. A petty autocrat, a narrow theocrat, or a corrupted fundamentalist. A person who thinks their way is the right way, and tells others to hit the highway. On a governmental level: Illegal surveillance, police-state thuggery. Persecution of dissidents. Fascism. Tyranny.

SYMBOLS:

- **Tornadoes:** Powerful ideas—ideas that may spin out of control
- **Magpie:** A very clever bird
- **Book:** Intellect, education
- **Fly:** Attention spent on inconsequential matters, or perhaps a little buzz

MINOR ARCANA

FUNGI • EARTH • PENTACLES • WEALTH • POSSESSIONS • CRAFT • TRADE

Ace of Fungi

An embroidered pink gauntlet floats in the cosmos. This gorgeous glove proudly presents us with an orange chanterelle bouquet of starry flowers and spiral fiddleheads. Multicolored bees swarm the lovely posies. A green caterpillar blends in with the ferns. Constellations of stars are plotted out and carefully labeled in the inky night sky.

INTERPRETATION:

The Ace of Fungi heralds an upcoming opportunity for prosperity. Be ready to act, and to receive the rewards created by your actions.

Upright: Go shake the money tree!

Opportunities for wealth materialize. This Ace is the power of prosperity, bringing security and riches. Be alert, stay focused, and financial success will follow.

Look for a lucrative contract or high-paying new job, a new business, or a skyrocketing investment. A very successful method of materializing profit is on the horizon. There are many paths to wealth: career success through cleverness and hard work is only the most obvious one.

MINOR ARCANA

FUNGI • EARTH • PENTACLES • WEALTH • POSSESSIONS • CRAFT • TRADE

The bees surrounding the bouquet testify to the sweetness of riches, but do not forget their sting; wealth comes with pain as well as pleasure.

Our culture has made greed into a virtue. Keep an eye on your hat size!

Reversed: Success is shaping up, but it is in its early days. Be patient and keep working. You are on the path to wealth. Or is an inheritance coming, the saddest way to acquire riches? Finally, could someone be swindling you?

SYMBOLS:

- **The cosmos:** As above, so below
- **Gauntlet:** The hand represents our ability to manipulate the outcome of events; the glove recommends employing subtlety, especially in business dealings. Sometimes it does not pay to be too direct.
- **Embroidery:** Craft, decoration, lovely things, attractive packaging
- **Sea daffodils:** Pure beauty
- **Bees:** Pollinators, fertility, sweetness, and sting
- **Fiddleheads:** Organic growth, spirals, the Fibonacci sequence
- **Caterpillar:** Life Is change.
- **Constellations:** Achieving and maintaining wealth requires far-reaching vision as well as organization.

Boadicea's Tarot of Earthly Delights

MINOR ARCANA

FUNGI • EARTH • PENTACLES • WEALTH • POSSESSIONS • CRAFT • TRADE

Two of Fungi

A woman with extra beetle-like appendages stands in the middle of a dirt path. Her (human) arms rest on her hips; her insect legs balance two large mushrooms above her shoulders. Her nipples bear golden stars.

The path behind her runs through a field of ripening wheat sprinkled with wildflowers. Against the horizon, a steeple rises above village roofs on the left, and a cozy farmhouse with a gently smoking chimney nestles into a hollow on the right.

INTERPRETATION:

The Two of Fungi encourages planning and balance in life and work.

Upright: It's time to take a more pragmatic approach. Juggling money, career, and lifestyle is currently a challenge. Take a deep breath, organize yourself, devise a formal budget, and consider your financial future. Where do you want to be in five years, or ten? You won't be able to keep juggling those mushrooms forever. As you get older, you may want a less physically challenging job—and you may also prefer to wear a shirt to work.

FUNGI • EARTH • PENTACLES • WEALTH • POSSESSIONS • CRAFT • TRADE

Reversed: Although you've tried various career paths, you have yet to find the best niche for your talents. Do not permit past failures to discourage you. You have many abilities. Versatility is a key to creating wealth. What can you do to move toward a rosier financial future? Think creatively. What do people want that you are willing and able to provide?

With organization and planning, you can find a route to material security.

SYMBOLS:

- **Tumbling mushrooms:** Dynamic balance, infinity symbol (lemniscate)
- **Church and cottage:** Spiritual vs. practical matters
- **Ripening wheat:** Reaping the results of wise decisions

FUNGI • EARTH • PENTACLES • WEALTH • POSSESSIONS • CRAFT • TRADE

Three of Fungi

A box turtle steadily approaches a group of workers erecting a faerie ring. The turtle is delivering more mushrooms to delineate the circle, under the self-appointed supervision of three snails.

It is the height of midsummer. The meadow grass is green, and tall cumulus clouds fill the sky. Does it look like it might rain later this afternoon?

INTERPRETATION:

Success in the early phases of a prestigious project. Things are starting to come together. You have laid a strong foundation.

Upright: Your crew is assembled and the work has begun. Collaboration and teamwork are crucial for your endeavors to succeed. Team wrangling is an essential function in complex projects. Conscientious oversight, a clear chain of command, and shared goals will lead to success, even triumph.

If everything continues as planned, the faerie circle will be lovely, and the faerie gala will be a spectacular success.

FUNGI • EARTH • PENTACLES • WEALTH • POSSESSIONS • CRAFT • TRADE

Reversed: It's hard to be patient when officious intermeddlers get right up your nose. Hang in there. This project is worthy of your efforts—and that's why so many busybodies have involved themselves.

If you encounter obstacles—don't permit yourself to be helpless, like a box turtle on its back. When plans go awry, it's time for a new approach.

If you are stuck in an unrewarding job, consider your options and make a plan. Stick your head out of your shell and look around: transporting toadstools to build faerie circles is not the only career possibility available.

SYMBOLS:

- **Fairy ring:** The work in progress, creating sacred space for a ritual dance
- **Box turtle:** Steady advancement, a reliable collaborator, an elder
- **Snails:** Earth spirits, time spirals, welcome aides, and, sometimes, pesky busybodies

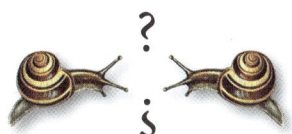

MINOR ARCANA

FUNGI • EARTH • PENTACLES • WEALTH • POSSESSIONS • CRAFT • TRADE

Four of Fungi

A self-satisfied person is seated in his study. With one proprietary hand he balances a huge ball of mushrooms on his lap. He gesticulates toward another mass of fungi with a pointed stick.

All manner of vanitas objects clutter the desk: a scroll, a pipe, a skull, glass vessels, ropes of pearls, an elaborate gold clock, marble statuettes, a busy black beetle, and a cryptic note. Four prize mushroom specimens bedeck this collection, and four soap bubbles float above all. The study walls are decorated with natural-history prints and an allegorical illustration of America personified as a naked woman riding an armadillo while cannibals go about preparing dinner in the middle distance.

INTERPRETATION:

This fellow has collected ALL the mushrooms, but will he share?

Upright: Stability created by material wealth and possessions. Having enormous amounts of stuff. Considering financial success a virtue. Inheriting property from family; trading on family prestige for individual advancement. Working hard as a self-made entrepreneur and then harshly judging others less able to make money. Beware smug

FUNGI • EARTH • PENTACLES • WEALTH • POSSESSIONS • CRAFT • TRADE

self-satisfaction. This goes double for anyone whose mushroom collection comes to them more easily as a result of privilege, such as male privilege, white privilege, or straight privilege. There are psychologically damaging illusions of personal superiority found among the upper crusts of all human societies. If you are successful, who helped you? How can you help raise others up to your level?

Reversed: Selfishness, greed, hoarding. The misconception that possessions ensure security. Anxiety over material loss. Stinginess, unwillingness to share, delusions that wealth equals virtue.

Judging yourself or others exclusively by net worth is quite common but should not be normal.

SYMBOLS:

- **Assorted possessions:** Material wealth and status
- **Skull:** Memento mori, "remember you must die" and leave all your stuff behind
- **Soap bubbles:** Life's fleeting pleasures
- **Cannibals:** Some people devour others with nary a pang of conscience, and in so many diverse ways.
- **America, a Personification**: Taste in art varies widely.

America, a Personification (ca. 1590)

A Dutch print depicting a female personification of the continent of North America, engraved by Flemish designer and engraver Adriaen Collaert after a design by Maerten de Vos. *Public Domain Revue*

Boadicea's Tarot of Earthly Delights 161

FUNGI • EARTH • PENTACLES • WEALTH • POSSESSIONS • CRAFT • TRADE

Five of Fungi

Is this an exterior or interior of a Christian church? A large stained-glass window casts multicolored light on the stone steps. The window's design presents five golden mushrooms dancing above depictions of medieval musicians, shepherds (with sheep), and what appears to be a fallen monarch.

Three figures cluster in front of the window. A girl in her early teens gently holds the arm of a gray-bearded man. His coat is worn; he leans on a cane and holds out his upturned hat. A shaggy, midsized mutt sits on a ledge behind them.

INTERPRETATION:

With the support of family, friends, and faith, we can weather hard times.

Upright: Financial insecurity, excessive debt, inadequate income. Your personal fortune is waning at this time. It's not a good time to take risks with money, or to spend frivolously. Look to your support networks for help. Think creatively, act sensibly, and you will be able to master your financial situation over time. Do not delay. Financial issues never get

FUNGI • EARTH • PENTACLES • WEALTH • POSSESSIONS • CRAFT • TRADE

better when they are ignored or denied. With self-discipline and patience, with help from friends, family, and community, your personal fortune can improve.

Reversed: You are falling into poverty. If you are threatened with homelessness, act now to mitigate the harm. Ask for help. There is no shame in asking your community to help you in times of dire need. However, you may have some disillusioning experiences with family and friends when you ask for help. If so, it says more about them, and not so much about you.

SYMBOLS:

- **Stained-glass church window:** Divine mercy, the comfort of faith, inspired craft
- **Stone steps:** They may appear intimidating, but they can lead you out of dire straits when tackled one at time.
- **Window imagery:** Musical trio–harmony; Shepherds–simple faith, hard work; Deposed king–even the mighty may fall on hard times.
- **Old man, young girl:** Stages of life, familial bonds, the quality of mercy
- **Dog:** Unconditional love

MINOR ARCANA

FUNGI • EARTH • PENTACLES • WEALTH • POSSESSIONS • CRAFT • TRADE

Six of Fungi

A negotiation is in progress. An impoverished man kneels at the feet of a man wearing a fine cloak trimmed with fur and gold fringe, and a snazzy snail-shell hat.

The wealthy man is engaged in a heated debate with a third figure, a minion or employee, who gestures toward a nearby cave mouth.

Two workers enter the cave, one carrying a large mushroom. It is apparent that some sort of fungi-farming project is in the works. The rich man is in a position to give the kneeling man a job. The underling is encouraging his boss to go for it.

INTERPRETATION:

Gone are the days of poverty! Through good fortune, gainful employment, or the good graces of a benefactor, you are back on the path to a more comfortable situation. Now is a good time to share those riches.

Upright: A new career opportunity. Financial security, material comfort. Charity, or a generous gift. Will you give, receive, or both? Owners and investors who share wealth generously with lower-level employees build

FUNGI • EARTH • PENTACLES • WEALTH • POSSESSIONS • CRAFT • TRADE

stronger companies. Contented employees work harder and are more loyal. Communities thrive when companies pay living wages, and when wealthy people are public-spirited enough to recognize that their generosity improves the environment.

Once the mushroom farm in the cave really gets going, everyone involved should benefit. Some enterprising mushroom farms are co-op businesses, or nonprofit organizations. Pursuing profit exclusively for personal gain does not provide a rich life. Lifting up impoverished people is a blessing for the givers as well as for those who receive.

Reversed: Better financial times are coming, but not yet. Continue to work hard, and be patient.

Which roles in this card image are you playing? Are you handling your role in business with integrity and skill? What changes could you make to work toward a splendid fungal triumph?

SYMBOLS:

- **Blue sky and a white dove:** Hope for a more prosperous future
- **Cavern mouth:** Mother Earth
- **Wheelbarrow:** Tools required for work, balance; you must hold up your end if you want to get anywhere.
- **Wheel:** What goes around comes around, you know. . .
- **Hedgehog:** A little urchin or earth spirit

MINOR ARCANA

FUNGI • EARTH • PENTACLES • WEALTH • POSSESSIONS • CRAFT • TRADE

Seven of Fungi

Seven large mushrooms have sprung up from the dirt floor of a cave. Every cap bears a human face, each with a different expression. The farmer stands with one hand on her hip and one on her chin, inspecting the mushrooms skeptically.

The cavern floor is dotted with more mushrooms, many almost ready for harvest. The cave's wide mouth opens onto the rocky coast of a calm lake. Farther down the shore, gentle waves lap at the walls of a stone castle.

INTERPRETATION:

What have we here? Those spores you scattered are ripening into fruit. Are the results what you had in mind? (Remember: there's always going to be some kind of beetle or other in every plan.)

Upright: You have worked diligently. If you continue to follow through, you can look forward to income from your toil. Forthcoming profit created by hard work and successful long-term planning. Your project will soon come to fruition; your scheme is on the verge of success. Soon you will reap the rewards for your work.

FUNGI • EARTH • PENTACLES • WEALTH • POSSESSIONS • CRAFT • TRADE

You formed a rock-solid plan and found a hospitable environment providing everything mushrooms need. You scattered the spores, and now you are on the verge of meeting, even exceeding, your goals. The castle of financial security is just a bit farther down the shore. Continue to do what's working well for you. You'll get there.

Reversed: Disappointment with poor return on investment. Unmet expectations, after some degree of work. Incredulity at unexpected results. Failure to evaluate business environment or marketability accurately. Or could this poor harvest be a result of inadequate effort?

SYMBOLS:

- **Lakeside cave:** Shelter, a good place to grow mushrooms
- **Lake:** Unconscious mind, whence inspiration emerges
- **Sandy beach leading to rocks:** Minute steps taken, sand grain by sand grain, rock by rock, to form a cave over geologic time, a sheltered and hospitable environment for founding a mushroom farm
- **Castle:** Financial security
- **Mushrooms:** Fruit of the earth, produced through consistent long-term hard work
- **Beetle:** Imperfection, a minor annoyance

MINOR ARCANA

FUNGI • EARTH • PENTACLES • WEALTH • POSSESSIONS • CRAFT • TRADE

Eight of Fungi

In an artist's studio where one wall is lined with plaster casts of dismembered sculptures, we see torsos, hands, faces, and a foot or two. An oil painting in progress rests on an easel. The artist has just paused to look up while sketching some colorful mushrooms. They appear to be a self-created manifestation of their own art, with the body of Apollo and the head of Venus.

INTERPRETATION:

You have mastered your craft.
You are at one with your art. Your life and your life's work are deeply felt expressions of your individuality. You yourself are your own most profound creation.

Upright: Well-earned accolades, productivity, highly developed skills, drive, and dedication. Your creativity brings you emotional satisfaction and material reward. You are recognized for your expertise in your field.

The focus and hard work required to be an entrepreneur, a person who can deliver on their commitments and meet deadlines too. Successfully turning an avocation into a vocation. More than a master of your craft, you have sculpted your own self, your persona, as subtly and beautifully as any of your other artworks.

FUNGI • EARTH • PENTACLES • WEALTH • POSSESSIONS • CRAFT • TRADE

Reversed: It is hard to be self-created. Now that you've broken the mold and emerged as your unique self, what comes next? You have a great foundation from which to express your creativity, but your skill level is not quite there yet. Meeting your goals will require more labor. Keep practicing and learning, and you will succeed. Or are your talents being overlooked or insufficiently rewarded?

SYMBOLS:

- **Artworks:** Creativity manifested
- **Head of Venus:** Roman Goddess of love, beauty, desire, and prosperity
- **Body of Apollo:** Greek God of music, healing, enlightenment, and light
- **Painting in progress:** The Queen of Fungi

MINOR ARCANA

FUNGI • EARTH • PENTACLES • WEALTH • POSSESSIONS • CRAFT • TRADE

Nine of Fungi

A woman both rich and beautiful stands in her lush walled garden. She holds her hawk on her arm. Luscious fruits and a bottle of ruby-red wine are arrayed on the balustrade, waiting for her to indulge.

She is dressed in moss-green velvet topped off by a jaunty chanterelle chapeau. Behind her, a sprawling hill-top castle overlooks fertile farmland. It is early evening, and the sky is the color of apricots.

Her hawk has the face of a handsome young man, which testifies to her ability to enchant her lovers. But with his hood off, the hawk-man seems distracted by a passing bumblebee. Is this a warning? Is she overestimating her ability to beguile him?

INTERPRETATION:

She appears to have everything. Is everything enough?

Upright: Prosperity, even wealth, bringing security and comfort. Your financial situation is coming together nicely. Will drowsing in the lap of luxury fulfill your fondest hopes and dreams over your entire lifetime? Or is your walled garden a retreat that sustains you after challenging labor, an oasis of calm amid chaos?

FUNGI • EARTH • PENTACLES • WEALTH • POSSESSIONS • CRAFT • TRADE

Those among us able to create wealth for ourselves have a responsibility to give back to our communities and to lift our communities up, a responsibility often ignored in modern society.

Reversed: Dissatisfaction, despite wealth. Unhappiness with the status quo, without any idea about how to change the situation. Relying on another for security, comfort, and happiness. Luxurious domestication.

Now that you have everything you need, what more do you want? What comes next? And what about your pet hawk? Does your financial security depend on him, with his possibly wandering eye? Or, unexpected financial rearrangements bringing diminished circumstances.

SYMBOLS:

- **Tethered hawk:** Wild nature tamed, restricted freedom
- **Castle on a hill:** Wealth and comfort
- **Melons, figs, and grapes:** Abundance, bountiful harvest
- **Wine:** Sensual pleasure, luxury, intoxication
- **Stone balustrade:** Order, enforced boundaries, property and propriety
- **Bee:** There it is again, representing the existential question

MINOR ARCANA

FUNGI • EARTH • PENTACLES • WEALTH • POSSESSIONS • CRAFT • TRADE

Ten of Fungi

Standing at the edge of a waterfall-fed pond, a family joyously regards their beautiful new home. The patriarch holds the deed of sale, as two people await the family's arrival by the front entrance.

The house is a handsome half-timbered edifice, with a tall mushroom-capped turret. Ten mushrooms tumble cheerfully down from the clear blue sky, landing in the pond with a glorious splash.

INTERPRETATION:

Behold! You have arrived!
The home of your dreams is now yours!

Upright: Home ownership. Material security, even luxury. Beauty, comfort, and joy. Truly belonging where you are, being part of a safe and loving family. Being loved, accepted, and appreciated by your biological or chosen family. A financial windfall, a successful investment, a family-owned company bought out by a bigger business. Multigenerational wealth passing from parent to child to grandchild. Normally, it takes several generations' worth of work to set up conditions for mushrooms to fall from the sky.

FUNGI • EARTH • PENTACLES • WEALTH • POSSESSIONS • CRAFT • TRADE

Reversed: Are you overburdened with material possessions, or excessive familial responsibilities? What steps could you take to free yourself? It's far easier to declutter than to delegate family needs, however. Do you feel stuck in the wrong place, or with the wrong people? It's hard to feel unappreciated. Sometimes, this describes a dysfunctional, even unsafe, family. Is it possible that you are contributing to your own problems? If so, what could you do to change that?

SYMBOLS:

- **Flying fungi:** Things falling into place, money coming out of the blue
- **Forceful waterfall:** Money increases the pressure on any lurking emotional issues within families.
- **Pond:** Abundant resources, enough for everyone, go with the flow
- **Children:** A family's future, happiness, familial love, multigenerational wealth
- **Fluffy little white dog:** Joyous companionship

MINOR ARCANA

FUNGI • EARTH • PENTACLES • WEALTH • POSSESSIONS • CRAFT • TRADE

Page of Fungi

A young lady wearing a fabulous fungi hat sits surrounded by cascading bouquets of flowers and fruit. Her arm is draped over a plump mushroom, and she holds an apple in her hand. Slugs crawl across her hat, and a hedgehog perches on her lap.

INTERPRETATION:

The lovely Page of Fungi heralds the start of a new financial enterprise. She brings the riches of the earth with her, along with her prickly companion.

Upright: Good news regarding money, a raise, a new job, or a surprisingly good earnings quarter. A new or emerging market for your products.

    A young person who appreciates the good things in life and has a cheerful willingness to work. A dedicated student, a focused, goal-oriented striver, someone who wants to learn now so they can earn later.

    Commencing job training that leads to more money. An apprentice of any age learning a new discipline. Older hedgehogs can indeed learn new and profitable tricks.

FUNGI • EARTH • PENTACLES • WEALTH • POSSESSIONS • CRAFT • TRADE

Reversed: Unpleasant financial news.

As a person, some reversed Pages of Fungi have been given everything, with the result that they value nothing. This type of person often assumes they are successful because of personal qualities, without acknowledging their privilege.

Or if the person described by this card is relatively poor, they are sometimes embittered and envious of wealthier kindred.

Lofty ambitions come to fruition only with hard work.

SYMBOLS:

- **Abundant flowers, fruit, and grains:** Productivity leading to prosperity
- **Pearls:** Rare, lovely, valuable, although they are the product of a poor mollusc's irritation
- **Apple:** The fruit of knowledge of wealth and poverty
- **Hat slugs:** Strangely stylish accessories; sometimes wealth brings slimy issues along with it.
- **Hedgehog:** Earth spirit, urchin, a prickly pet. Wealth requires firm personal boundaries, or it doesn't last long.

FUNGI • EARTH • PENTACLES • WEALTH • POSSESSIONS • CRAFT • TRADE

Knight of Fungi

The Knight of Fungi's snail-shell helmet covers a hard head for business. He is an unpretentious and down-to-earth individual.

Although perched comically askew on his humble brown steed, this knight is a more formidable adversary than he looks. He quite competently fends off several predatory con men with one dismissive wave of his magic mushroom.

Trust, especially in financial matters, needs to be earned.

INTERPRETATION:

The Knight of Fungi and his noble steed Balthazar gallantly protect your financial stability and material goods. They advise you to be prudent, but not stingy, in your dealings with others.

Upright: Your finances are well protected and well served.

What can you do to further your own professional advancement today? It's a good time to seek a new job, ask for a raise, or make a long-term investment.

Or here is an honest trustee, an honorable employee or business partner. This is a responsible person, someone trustworthy with money and other valuables, someone who will follow the law exactly. He is the least dashing but the most reliable Knight.

FUNGI • EARTH • PENTACLES • WEALTH • POSSESSIONS • CRAFT • TRADE

Reversed: Read the fine print. Are you sure the contract says exactly what you think? Financial matters are not progressing smoothly. Progress may be stalled, or bad financial news may be forthcoming. Inertia replaces business progress; plans fall apart; quarterly earnings are low.

This reversed Knight is dishonest, a treacherous agent, a con artist. Trusting him or depending upon him is a mistake. Or, could there be an embezzler at work?

SYMBOLS:

- **Dubious characters:** Threats to your livelihood
- **Coins and dice:** Gambling, risk
- **Fruiting mosses:** Earthly prosperity

FUNGI • EARTH • PENTACLES • WEALTH • POSSESSIONS • CRAFT • TRADE

Queen of Fungi

The Queen leans back against a mossy mound, her black hair and white shoulders framed by the upstanding collar of her bejeweled cloisonné capelet. She wears a gown of frilly, gilly orange chanterelle mushrooms. Her bare feet rest within an enchanted mushroom ring, while a screen of iris creates a backdrop for her living throne.

INTERPRETATION:

The Queen of Fungi loves to be surrounded by beauty and abundance.

How people react to this Queen says a great deal about their inner struggles with issues of money and prosperity.

Upright: Intelligence focused on pragmatic matters. A bountiful harvest. The rewards of wise investments.

A practical, generous person. Someone who can afford their good taste, and who enjoys being surrounded by beautiful, even luxurious things.

FUNGI • EARTH • PENTACLES • WEALTH • POSSESSIONS • CRAFT • TRADE

Deeply rooted in her earthly realm, this gracious Queen enjoys sharing through generous hospitality, patronage of the arts, and nurturing the careers of protégés. She resonates with the earth's bounty like a human manifestation of The Empress: material comfort, beauty, and financial security are her gifts.

Her wealth and beauty, her generosity and good taste, inspire gratitude, envy, accusations of elitism, deep appreciation, love—and many imitators.

Reversed: A greedy or materialistic person. A relentless social climber. Acquisitive hoarding. Dissatisfaction, despite material comfort. Poor taste, foolish spending.

In reversal, this Queen cares too much for possessions and status symbols. She's never met a wealthy person she disliked, nor a poor one she cared for.

SYMBOLS:

- **Iris:** Fleur-de-lis, trinity, threefold rule, Greek goddess of the rainbow
- **Cloisonné cape and chanterelle gown:** Beautiful, beautiful beauty
- **Bare feet:** Connection to nature
- **Fairy circle:** Earth magic

FUNGI • EARTH • PENTACLES • WEALTH • POSSESSIONS • CRAFT • TRADE

King of Fungi

The King braces himself against a great boulder and raises his mushroom scepter to the sky. His dark eyes flash beneath his golden helmet. His scarlet cloak unfurls, revealing his powerful body. His physical strength and determined will are immediately evident; his rational nature requires a little more insight to comprehend.

INTERPRETATION:

Here is a practical ruler, with a deeply rooted command of the material realm. Although he appreciates property and wealth, he does not permit avarice to cloud his commitment to a higher purpose.

Upright: Stability, common sense, prudence. Good financial management. This King has the knowledge and understanding to work with wealth wisely.

The King of Fungi is the monarch of worldly goods. Whether their goods are inherited or earned, people who resonate with this King make sure they are not poor. They tend to focus on long-term, conservative investments and dislike excessive financial risk. This King very rarely

FUNGI • EARTH • PENTACLES • WEALTH • POSSESSIONS • CRAFT • TRADE

shades into outright greed. He is a person of integrity and immense common sense, grounded in material reality, someone who can be trusted with money and other valuables.

Reversed: Delay or denial of financing. Sketchy business practices. Bad management. Ignorance or oblivion in practical matters. This grifter King schemes his way to profit. He uses his skills and authority to make shady or outright corrupt deals, and to exploit others for financial gain. Do not trust him with money or keys, and definitely not with your heart!

SYMBOLS:

- **Mountains:** Bones of the earth
- **Golden helmet (with fungal plume):** Prowess as a warrior and protector
- **Cloth of gold and scarlet:** Royal raiment
- **Many mushrooms:** Material wealth

LAGNIAPPE

∞ : Perspicacious Platypus

A platypus regards their reflection in a large, ornate gilt-framed mirror. The mirror leans against a wall covered with indigo wallpaper, representing outer space. It is sprinkled with thousands of tiny stars. Left of the mirror hang three framed portraits: a duck, a beaver, and a photograph of Pamela Coleman Smith.

The vision in the mirror is a bold contrast to the subdued room decor. Our platypus happily regards their double in the looking glass rising from a lush garden. Exuberant blossoms burst from the beds, blanketing the greenery with impressionistic hues. In the near distance a sassy Venus statue gazes toward the platypus across a lily pond.

The platypus and their reflection smile proudly at each other. A shaft of rainbow light falls from beyond the mirror, passing through the mirror's crowning ornament of the All Seeing Eye, and angles through the garden to bathe the platypus in all the colors of love.

INTERPRETATION:

Upright: This platypus (representing the reader or querent) has achieved a very personal enlightenment; perhaps through study of Tarot, perhaps through life experience. They have learned to know themselves and love themselves: as they are, as they have been, and as they will be. They have come to accept themselves for both their inner shadows and their inner light. This understanding brings joy and peace. Self-acceptance allows them to accept others with forgiveness and affection. We are all multifaceted, imperfect, inspiring, exasperating, lovable, all too mortal beings.

Reversed: Now the platypus is upended, finding themself in a not-dissimilar predicament as The Hanged Man: experiencing an inner existential crisis. The platypus is working through where to "go" with themselves; what to embrace and what to leave behind. Instead of knowing and loving themselves, they are still looking to others for guidance as they weigh their sense of self.

Yet, revelation is imminent—they are poised to plunge into a rainbow pool—their physical and spiritual selves finally in harmony. This card, in reversal, advises deep soul-searching. Be realistic and work to love yourself as you are, in all your messy human glory.

Know yourself and love yourself! (And remember: fully adult spiritual beings know how to behave themselves for best results.)

SYMBOLS:

- **Platypus:** An amphibious marsupial found in Australia and New Zealand
- **Perspicacity:** Possessing acute mental awareness and discernment
- **Duck and beaver portraits:** When first encountered by Europeans, the platypus was thought to be a taxidermy assemblage of a beaver and a duck.
- **Golden mirror:** A portal framed in love and glory; Perspective number one: let your self-examination be tempered with love and acceptance
- **Celestial Wallpaper:** It's an infinite universe out there. Other perspective number one: cultivate humility while you are regarding yourself. Look to the Temperance card to find balance.
- **The All Seeing Eye**: is looking through you, just as you are looking through it.
- **Venus:** Goddess of love and beauty
- **The Garden:** Your inner Eden
- **Rainbow ray:** Love is love.
- **Pamela Coleman Smith (a.k.a. "Pixie"):** The genius artist who created the interpretive imagery for the Rider-Waite-Smith Tarot deck, first published in 1909

Reading the Cards
The Spirit of Inquiry

*How to phrase the question is
often just as important as the question itself.*

Divination literally means "to be inspired by a divinity," an activity found in all human societies dating from the most-ancient times. Divination is the act of using an occult system designed to provide insight into a question or situation, a way to consult the Gods and spirits, a symbolic method of analyzing the tenor of the times we live in.

There are innumerable systems of divination. The Tarot is a comparatively modern one. Tarot cards as a divination system descend from a gambling game played by the aristocracy starting in northern Italy around 1450 or so. It was not until much later, in France in the 1780s, that Antoine Court de Gébelin and "Etteilla," the pseudonym of Jean-Baptiste Alliette, suggested working with Tarot cards for divination instead of gambling, using the Tarot de Marseilles.

Tarot cards were mostly a continental European phenomenon and were not common in the English-speaking world until a bit more than a hundred years ago. In 1910, A. E. Waite and Pamela Colman Smith produced the Rider-Waite-Smith (RWS) deck, the first Tarot deck to become widely popular and easily available in the English-speaking world. The RWS deck is still one of the most beloved Tarots in the world today. *Boadicea's Tarot of Earthly Delights* is based on Pamela Colman Smith's masterful artwork. Her illustrations follow the occult system that A. E. Waite devised, drawing on the teachings of the Hermetic Order of the Golden Dawn, an occult secret society active in London during that era.

⊙⊙⊙ ✦ ⊙⊙⊙

Here are nine suggestions on how to get the best results in divination. Getting helpful results in divination sometimes depends on phrasing your question effectively. It's an art and a skill to phrase questions in ways that elicit solid divinatory information.

DIVINATION

1. Do not ask an either/or pair as a single question.
A pair of choices is actually two questions: What is likely to happen if I pursue course of action A? What is likely to happen if I pursue course of action B? If you ask something like "Should I go with A or B?," the answer is liable to be confusing, especially with a one-card reading.

2. Ask "quality" questions, not "quantity" questions, "how" not "when."
For example, if asking about the potential for a future relationship with a specific person, a question such as, "If I begin a romantic relationship with X, what would that be like for me?" tends to elicit information that is truly helpful in decision-making.

3. Be as specific as possible.
For example, if you are planning a move and you are not sure where you want to live next, one possible way to phrase that is, "Please show me what is likely to occur if I move to X location" and then pull one card. Pull a single card for each location you are considering, and compare them.

4. When we ask the Tarot to answer a question, the cards are describing the most probable future course of events on the basis of the current situation.
The cards we receive in answer to a question describe the most likely probabilities manifesting from current events.

5. Do not ask about soulmates.
Phrasing the question that way instantly games the results, because there is no one person who is perfect for each of us, in my long-held opinion. Especially do not ask when you will meet a soulmate. Instead, consider asking what you can do to attract a compatible partner, if that is what you are hoping to do.

Also, consider asking the Tarot to suggest what you yourself might do, in terms of personal shadow work, that would help you prepare yourself for a happy partnership.

Tarot is a superb metaphysical tool for helping us see and integrate our shadow selves. Tarot can be your partner in personal psychological work, the lifelong work of compassion and healing for self and others. Working with Tarot as a spiritual practice can help us make progress toward happiness, wholeness, and fulfillment and help us move away from lingering PTSD, depression, and patterns of self-sabotage.

6. Do not ask when a person will die, period.
It's not a good question. Normally this question results in confusing answers, since there are enormous numbers of variables.

7. Do not become angry at the cards (or a diviner) if the answers you are getting from the cards do not make you happy.
If you don't want to know home truths, do not ask leading questions. Pleasant platitudes and comforting lies do not help people make progress in compassion for self and others.

8. Do not ask the same question over and over again.
Unfortunately, most people do this because they didn't like the first answer and are hoping the answer will change. This is a type of bargaining, and it does not work, simply put.

9. Keep your questions tightly focused.
Asking very broad questions generally results in less useful information. There is too much variability at that level for the cards to give useful answers.

Here we are at the very dawn of a new aeon. We are the people setting up the paradigm in the first moments of a 2,000-year cycle. Birthing the Aquarian Age is an important responsibility, so let's do the best job we can.

Boadicea's Tarot of Earthly Delights can help us set the stage for our descendants yet to come. *Boadicea's Tarot* is a sophisticated wisdom tool designed as a beautiful pack of cards. If you work with this deck faithfully and with integrity, you can make progress in your life that will change the course of your own future, and the future of the descendants yet to come, biological and spiritual.

Our acts, birthed in this time and place, will affect the descendants no matter who we become, no matter what we do. Let us move forward into the future with clear-sighted courage, compassion, and wisdom.

It is increasingly obvious that humanity needs a massive course correction. Let's cut to the chase and act to diminish future sorrows today, guided by *Boadicea's Tarot of Earthly Delights*.

Reading Tarot
Reading Tarot Is an Art

Ground yourself, breathe, and center your energy. Concentrate on a question, your own or a querent's. Shuffle the deck, in whatever method you prefer, until the cards feel nicely mixed. Cut the cards, pick up your piles, and deal. Look at each card image, read the meaning, and analyze the card for synchronicities with the question.

Beginners should start with one question, one card, and slowly move to two or three cards per question. Complicated spreads with lots of cards can be confusing, especially for less experienced readers.

Over time, it helps people to follow a routine for reading Tarot. Choose a particular way to cut the cards. Choose a particular place for reading, with room to lay the cards out comfortably. Many people like to have a crystal, a seashell, or a lit candle on their reading surface. Some like reading cloths; others prefer a wooden table. These sorts of mildly ritualized framings help readers move from mundane consciousness toward a single-minded focus on the cards.

Keep a Tarot Journal.
While learning, faithfully pull a card a day from your deck. Then write a few sentences or phrases about the correspondences between the Tarot card, and what actually takes place that day.

Keeping a journal permits review of the readings. Consider reviewing the journal monthly and annually, looking for the flow of synchronicities in the readings.

Deepening Reading Skills
The best way to learn the cards: play with them. Lay various arrangements of cards out on a reading table and contemplate the card images.

Lay out the Ace through Ten in each suit and note how the story arc flows.

Lay out the four Aces and consider them as a group, while contemplating their similarities and their differences. Then lay out the four Twos, and so on.

Lay out the four Pages and compare their similarities and differences across suits. Do this for all the court cards.

Match the The Magician with the four Aces, The High Priestess with the four Twos, and so on. How do these numbers resonate across the five card images and meanings?

Separate the Majors from your deck. Lay out The Fool at the top of a large reading table. Below her, lay out three rows of seven Majors each, in numerical order. Compare/contrast the seven cards, beginning with The Magician and ending with The Chariot. Follow the card meanings across all three rows of seven. This is of The Journey of The Fool.

Then scrutinize the three rows of seven cards vertically, starting with The Magician, Strength, and The Devil, through The Chariot, Temperance, and The World.

Consider Iconography across the Entire Deck

Lay out the entire deck in order. Analyze the natural phenomena in the cards.

Look at the light in the cards: Where does the light come from in the image? Consider the symbolic messages carried by clouds, rainbows, lightning, lava, and aurorae. There are many cards showing the moon: compare and contrast them.

Which cards are interior scenes and which take place in nature? How does being indoors or outdoors affect esoteric associations with the scene?

What kind of plants and animals are in the card image, and how do they support the card meaning?

Where are the Tarot characters looking in the card illustrations? Do the characters look at the observer, or are their eyes looking elsewhere? How does the direction of the character's gaze influence the image?

How is the elemental association of the suit presented in the cards? Which cards show another element alongside images of the ruling element?

These smaller increments of the card designs subtly enrich and support the symbolic meanings. The Symbols section of the card meanings is very important.

Journal Your Compare/Contrast Exercises

For the gold standard of Tarot study: devote an entire journal to notes on the individual cards, and commentary about the suits and the Arcanas, rather than notes about your Tarot readings. Use sticky tabs and consider using a ring binder you can expand. File your notes under each card, not chronologically. This requires a large notebook.

Reading Styles

Tarot readers are at their best when reading cards in their favorite, most comfortable style. Some people like to choose a card representing the querent or the question, a significator, and others choose not to do so. Some readers interpret reversed cards, and others strive to deal all cards upright. Different readers look at the relationships among the cards in a reading differently.

Reading Cards with
Boadicea's Tarot of Earthly Delights

Please consider looking at "The Spirit of Inquiry" and "Reading Tarot," before working with the cards, especially if you are a beginner. Learning how to ask questions for divination is an art. For a quick start, here are some productive questions to consider.

"What is my next best step toward a better outcome?"

"What am I missing in this situation, or about this person's behavior?"

"Please show me the most likely outcome to this situation."

"Please show me the hidden agenda of this person or in this situation."

"Is this person lying to me?"

"What will I learn if I have a relationship with this person or get involved with this situation?"

These last several questions are particularly good ones to ask the cards when considering a new romantic prospect.

ONE CARD

Ask a question and pull a single card. One question, one card is the simplest, most essential way to divine with cards.

Card 1: This card is a symbolic answer to the question posed by the reader or querent.

Examine the symbolism and consider the card meaning. How might the card's divinatory meaning intersect with, or offer commentary upon, the question?

Now ask a follow-up question and pull another single card, if needed.

TWO CARDS

Ask a question and pull two cards. This reading gives information about the present and immediate future of a person or situation. Or, work with a pair of cards designated to symbolize any paired concept you prefer.

Card 1: This card represents a person or situation in the present.

Card 2: This card represents the probable immediate future of that person or situation.

THREE CARDS

An arrangement of three cards in a line is a favorite basic spread. The three card positions can be considered in any number of ways. Here are some frameworks for the three card positions.

PAST, PRESENT, AND FUTURE

Card 1 | The Past: This card mirrors the roots of a situation in the past. To truly understand the present, and to be able to see the future coming, we need to see the past very clearly.

Card 2 | The Present: This card shows what forces are operating at the present time in the situation in question. This card will sometimes reveal hidden or unexpressed aspects to a situation.

Card 3: | The Future: This card displays the most probable future of the situation or question.

SUBJECT, OBJECT, AND RELATIONSHIP

Card 1: This card represents the reader or querent.

Card 2: This card represents a friend or acquaintance.

Card 3: This card represents the relationship or potential relationship between the subject and the object.

BRILLIANCE, SHADOW, AND ALCHEMY

Card 1: This card symbolizes the public face of a person, or the stated purpose of an organization, an action, or a situation. This is what the person, action, situation, or organization is projecting.

Card 2: This card symbolizes the hidden purpose or concealed agenda motivating that person or situation. This card shows the shadow, whatever the person or the situation is concealing, whether consciously or unconsciously.

Card 3: This card symbolizes the alchemy between the projections and the shadow in synergy, the sum of the two, whether the combination is dignified and helpful, destructive and harmful, or—the most likely by far—a little bit of both.

WANT, NEED, AND ACT

Card 1: This card represents what I want.

Card 2: This card represents what I need.

Card 3: This card represents my next best step forward.

Feel free to assign your own set of meanings for this basic three-card spread.

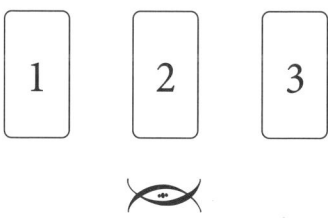

FIVE CARD CROSS VARIATIONS

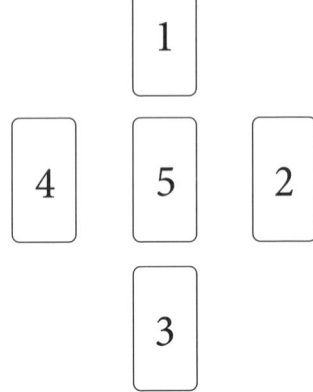

This five-card spread is endlessly useful. There are numerous ways to analyze the cards in this layout.

Deal five cards, starting from the top or north position, clockwise around the four compass points, with the final card at the center.

BOADICEA'S BADASSERY

Boadicea and her daughters suffered grave injustice at the hands of the Romans after King Prasutagus died. As a folk heroine and sacred ancestress, Boadicea's life story exemplifies a courageous woman who refused to be victimized.

This spread is designed to analyze situations of conflict and offer the reader suggestions on what they might do to improve the outcome.

Card 1 | The Conflict Situation: This card symbolizes the conflict situation, the subject of the reading.

Card 2 | Watch for It–the Back Stab: This card symbolizes any hidden betrayal or unseen weakness at the root of the conflict. This card often represents deception or self-sabotage, a vulnerability from within.

Card 3 | My Superpower: This card symbolizes the gifts, talents, and alliances that assist and strengthen the querent's position in the conflict.

Card 4 | What Would Boadicea Do? This card symbolizes the next best step the querent could take toward manifesting a better outcome for themselves.

Card 5 | Probable Outcome: If you find this outcome card unsatisfactory, if you don't like this potential outcome, refer back to the first four cards for hints about actions to take that might improve the situation and thus change the probable outcome.

THE SPIRIT SPREAD

Card 1 | Earth: This card represents the physical and material qualities of the person or situation. This card gives information about physical health and wealth, such as inheritance, property, and real estate.

Card 2 | Air: This card represents the mental aspects of the person or situation. This card gives information about personal and interpersonal communications, mental health or illness, or the group mind created by those involved in a situation.

Card 3 | Fire: This card represents the strength of character of a person or the power of a situation. This card gives information about the passion and will burning within a person, or the pivotal power of a situation to create change.

Card 4 | Water: This card represents the emotional nature of a person or a situation. This card gives information about the normal emotional state and the range of emotions for a person, or about the emotional development and the value of emotion within a group.

Card 5 | Spirit: This card provides archetypal information about the person or situation that is the focus of the reading. This card gives information about overarching resonances, commentary about a person's future path, or what type of future trajectory will manifest from a current situation.

Take careful note of the Spirit card, especially which suit and arcana it comes from. The center card is always very telling.

TIME AFTER TIME

Card 1: A person or situation now

Card 2: One month from now

Card 3: Three months from now

Card 4: Six months from now

Card 5: One year from now

There are any number of card placement meanings for the five-card spread. Feel free to assign your own card position meanings, and to deal the cards in whatever order you prefer.

MODERN CELTIC CROSS

This updated spread inspired by A. E. Waite's Ancient Celtic Method is useful for analyzing big questions or complicated, long-term situations.

Significator: Feel free to choose a significator from among the cards to represent the reader or the querent.

Card 1 | This Covers You: This card represents the general atmosphere around the focus of the reading. Whether the focus is yourself or a situation, the covering card gives a metaphor of the energies at work.

Card 2 | This Crosses You: This card symbolizes the energies arrayed in opposition to the cover card. This card is always read right side up. If this card is positive, it can help or soften the cover card rather than hindering it.

Card 3 | The Root of the Matter: This card is a metaphor for everything that is the foundation of the situation or at the heart of the inquiry.

Card 4 | The Past: This card describes energies that are ending or waning in the situation.

Card 5 | The Future: This card shows what will most probably happen in the future.

Card 6 | This Crowns You: This card shows something that may happen, but is not certain to happen in the situation.

Card 7 | Hopes and Fears: This card represents your hopes and fears in the matter.

Card 8 | Family and Friends: This card is a metaphor for the influences and energies of family and friends in the situation.

Card 9 | Dreams and Ideals: This card represents your dreams and ideals in the matter.

Card 10 | What Will Come: This card represents the outcome of the question, the progression of events in the situation, the end of the story.

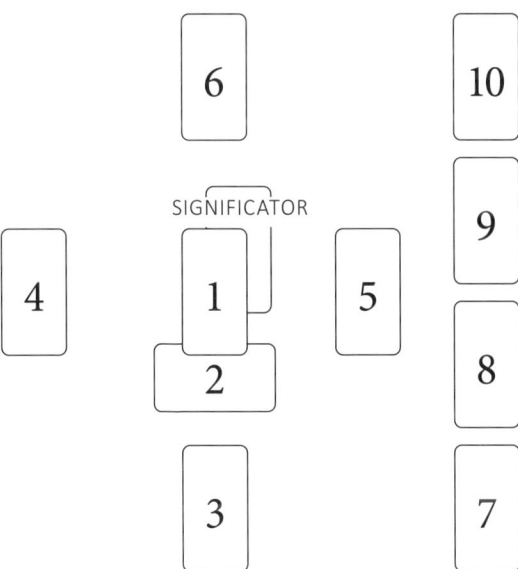

TAROT SPREADS

GRAND GARDEN OF EARTHLY DELIGHTS
Custom spread by Sara Mastros, The Fool's Dog

The Garden of Earthly Delights is a famous artwork, a three-part painting called a triptych, by fourteenth-century Flemish master Hieronymous Bosch, owned by the Prado museum in Madrid, Spain.

In the central panel, humans take pleasure and delight in manifest reality on Earth. In the left panel, God is shown, with Adam and Eve in the Garden of Eden. In the right panel, the consequences of human disobedience are shown in Hell. This painting forms the basis for this reading.

This spread gives a detailed overview of a situation, offering opportunities for strategic planning. This reading does not offer advice but, rather, presents intelligence about what is actually taking place, above board and beneath the surface.

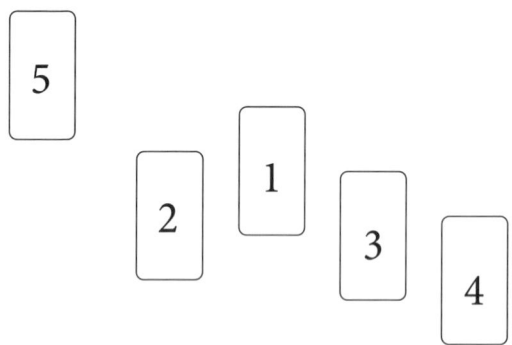

Card 1 | Situation: The situation at hand. This card shows the underlying nature of the person, force, or situation you are investigating.

Card 2 | Internal Basis: This card shows the character aspects or habitual response that sets the stage for this situation—hopes, fears, thoughts, or emotions about the situation.

Card 3 | External Basis: This card shows a person, force, or situation outside the reader or querent that is helping to bring about this situation. This card manifests aspects of the situation in the outside world: often showing other people's responses to the situation.

Card 4 | Hell: This card shows a person, force, or situation that is actively causing harm in this situation, if any. Look for ways to avoid, contain, or defuse the aspects of the situation described by this card. Often, just being aware of this facet of the situation is enough to dodge it.

Card 5 | Heaven: This card shows a person, force, or situation that is actively helping the person or the situation.

 This card identifies the main ally. Consider ways to work with this ally to your further advantage. This card describes the pivot point that will lead you to success.

BOADICEA'S CHARIOT
What awaits on the road ahead?

Custom spread by Sara Mastros, The Fool's Dog

Boadicea's name meant "Victory" in her Brittonic Celtic language. In her uprising against the Romans, Boadicea—whose name was probably closer to Boudicca—drove a war chariot with whirling, scythe-sharp blades into battle.

This spread is designed to investigate a project with a defined goal, such as getting a job or finding a new roommate or romantic partner. Working with the spread is most helpful in the planning stages, to help the project take form. The spread can also be very helpful when a project is stuck.

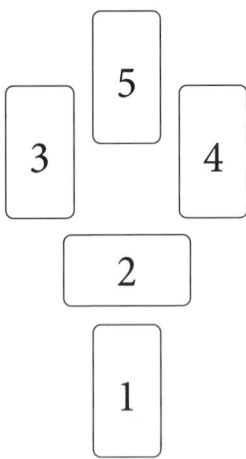

Card 1 | The Charioteer: This is the force that is driving or steering the project. This card can often provide insights about sneakiness, or hidden agendas in play.

Card 2 | The Chariot: This is the force that openly carries the project forward. The Chariot is the foundation of the enterprise. It represents something or someone already working within the situation: an individual, an organization, or a shared conviction guiding the work, for example.

(If the top of the card is to the left, read the card as upright. If the top of the card is on the right, read the card as reversed.)

The Two Horses

Card 3 | First Horse and Card 4 | Second Horse: The two horse cards should be read as a pair. Both represent the motivating energy driving the project forward. If the two cards are well dignified, for example, harmoniously in the same suit, the forces carrying the project forward are in alignment with one another. The end result may be for good or ill, but everyone involved is pulling in the same direction.

If the two horses are poorly dignified: for example, one is from Æther and the other from Fungi, or one is from Combustion and the other from Tentacles, that suggests that the project is being pulled in opposing directions, or that not everyone working together shares the same goals.

Card 5 | The Road Ahead: This card advises on the best action you can take to help the project succeed.

THE HAMSA OF PROTECTION
Custom spread by Sara Mastros, The Fool's Dog

This spread is based on the familiar metaphysical symbol of an eye in the palm of a hand. This is an ancient design found in many cultures and called a Hamsa in the Middle East. This spread is inspired by the Octo-Hamsa-pod on *Boadicea Tarot's* card back.

Traditionally, the Hamsa is considered especially potent at turning away the Evil Eye, the jealous gaze of someone ill-wishing another. The Hamsa literally turns the spiritual harm away, a type of design called apotropaic. So this spread is designed to investigate a dangerous opponent or an oppressive situation, and to reveal possible approaches to protecting the reader or querent from harm.

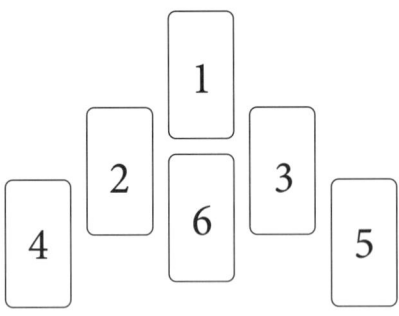

The Middle Finger

Card 1 | The Opponent: This card symbolizes the opposing forces, person, or situation that is the focus of the reading.

The Ring Finger

Card 2 | The Opponent's Ally: This card represents an external person, force, or situation that is supporting the negative situation.

The Index Finger

Card 3 | Self-Sabotage: This card represents the reader or querent's internalized psychic or spiritual wound: a thought, characteristic, habit, or emotion that supports or feeds into the bad situation.

The Pinkie Finger

Card 4 | Your Ally: This is the external handle on the situation.

This card describes a dependable ally, someone or something supporting the best aspects of the situation. Consider how to align with this ally to best advantage.

The Thumb

Card 5 | Your Gift: This card speaks to the internal ability or virtue in the situation. This is a talent, insight, gift, or emotion within the reader or querent that supports and protects them.

The All-Seeing Eye

Card 6 | Your Symbol: Within this card image, there is a symbol you can work with to protect yourself. This symbol will alert you to pay attention to potential danger when you see it again.

What part of the card jumped out to you when you first viewed it? In the future when you encounter this symbol, pause to consider how the immediate present might be related to this difficult situation.

This reading offers potent insight on how to break toxic personal patterns. It shows a pivot point for achieving long-term healing and protection from harm.

Be alert for the symbol, with the understanding that some people simply cannot stop themselves from jealousy or envy. Traditional cultures all believe in some type of evil eye, in which a person's envy or jealousy takes malignant form, manifesting misfortune in the object of that envy's life.

Protect yourself, or regrets to follow.

BOADICEA'S SAGA SPREAD
A Tale in Nine Cards

This simple layout, three rows of three cards each, is my favorite spread for reading about a complicated situation. It is also helpful for personal analysis, of self or others, when trying to understand the underlying motivations behind confusing or hurtful actions.

This spread is read as a story. All the cards relate to one another: be sure to contemplate the associations among the three vertical rows, as well as the three horizontal rows. Don't neglect the diagonal axes: they provide contrasting strains of meaning within the reading.

The only constant I've found with this layout: the center card describes the center of the story. Often, I have found that the card in the center surprises me in relation to the question or person.

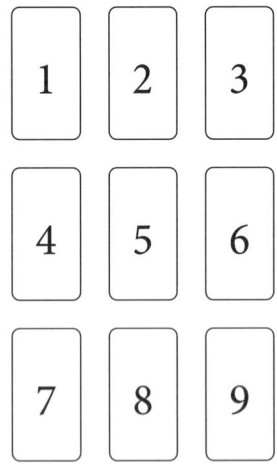

If you are brave enough to read about yourself, here's some advice. When you see the cards, if you don't like what you see, there is no use becoming defensive or angry. Just think about the images and the flow of the cards and ponder them, without reacting emotionally. Do the cards hold a home truth that you find insulting, but on consideration, you have to own the behavior described? That was certainly my experience.

We cannot correct what we do not see, or refuse to acknowledge. Boadicea's Saga can be a very helpful tool for self-analysis with an eye toward self-improvement.

This spread has also helped me when trying to understand the motivation behind someone's action that hurt or offended me. In such situations, this spread has helped me get past anger and find compassion for the other person every time. All too often when people act from their inner wounds, they hurt or offend other people.

Because this spread gives a symbolic portrait of a person, it reveals the subject's wounds and often permits a glimpse of the dysfunction motivating behavior that others find unpleasant or challenging.

This spread has also helped me understand what I may have done to trigger the behavior that hurt my feelings or offended me. I suggest using this spread to read about yourself, before considering reading about another person.

These are suggestions for phrasing the questions in four different types of readings with this Block of Nine layout.

- *Boadicea's Tarot,* please show me how people in my community see me, or how another specific person sees me.

- *Boadicea's Tarot,* please show me my limitations, my strengths, and my next best moves in life.

- *Boadicea's Tarot,* please show me the motivations of the person who hurt my feelings or offended me, or, please show me what is really happening in a situation that is challenging.

- *Boadicea's Tarot,* please show me the true agenda of a person or the motivating cause of a situation. What are the overt and covert agendas, and what is the outcome likely to be?

If you are very brave, ask this spread about yourself.

FINALLY

TAKE OFF THE TRAINING WHEELS AND GO!
Moving from Beginner to Intermediate, and on to Tarot Expert

The three main tasks of a Tarot beginner:
1. Memorize the card meanings and symbolism.
2. Learn to work with various spreads.
3. Record all readings in a journal.

Once you have memorized the cards, it's rewarding to experiment with different styles of reading. Trying different reading styles will help you determine the best ways to read Tarot for you personally.

Try different ways of shuffling and cutting the cards, until you find your most comfortable style. Read with/without a significator, and with/without card reversals. Try reading spreads as stories, with no assigned card positions. Journal everything. Over time, you will develop your preferred individual style of reading.

When you start devising your own spreads, here is a potentially helpful hint. Get a pack of index cards. Write your card position names on index cards and then lay out the index cards before you begin shuffling and laying out the Tarot cards. The prominent card position names help keep you focused on exactly what you are asking the Tarot to answer.

When reading Tarot for yourself, it is good practice to review your Tarot journals. Compare and contrast your readings with the events in your life. Some people read their Tarot journals for the past six months as part of their annual ritual cycle. The most popular time to review divination journals is at the equinoxes, because they are a time of solar balance.

There is only one metric to measure whether you are doing a good job reading Tarot: Do your Tarot readings for yourself help you? Do your Tarot readings help your friends and clients?

If your readings are helping you, or if your readings help other people, then you are indeed doing a good job with Tarot.

FINALLY

Tarot is a wisdom tool designed
as a game.

*Working with Tarot can help you understand yourself,
refine your goals, and achieve success and happiness.
Tarot deepens compassion for self and others.
Tarot enhances life.*

*Tarot helps us learn to re-enchant the world
and thus create a better future
for our descendants yet to come.*

Hail, Boadicea!

APPENDIX

The collage illustrations for *Boadicea's Tarot of Earthly Delights* are unique, transformative artworks. Each of the 81 collages is much more than the sum of its parts. Through extensive recombination and photo editing of the many components, original new works have been created. Each of the individual collages contains elements from at least five or six—and often up to as many as a dozen—different public-domain sources. Each card illustration is just one integral element of the entire Tarot deck entity.

With their quirky imagery and humorous juxtaposition of elements, the collages are presented as whimsical parodies of classical paintings, especially those works originally created to appeal to the robber barons and upper classes of America's Gilded Age. We hope you are both amused and delighted by this reinterpretation of the genre.

(Please note that these new compositions in no way imply the approval or intent of the original creators of the artworks or an endorsement of Boadicea Design LLC.)

IMAGE SOURCES AND CREDITS

* indicates {{PD-US-expired}}

Original drawings by Paula Millet: fiddle-head ferns; firefly; moon yoyo; infinity symbol.

Photos by Paula Millet: pillared gazebo, Nashville, Tennessee; stone gate at Gillette Castle State Park, Hadlyme, Connecticut; a dog's teeth; statuette of the *Venus di Milo;* narwhal toy; forest background; chains; steak knife blades; grandmother's pocket watch; toy platypus; picture frames; carpet; footstool; other miscellaneous items.

From the personal vintage print collection of Paula Millet: Pre-1924 anatomical lithographs of the eye and the hand.

Contributed photos: Vultures by Tom Lehr; Phoenix, Arizona sunset by Michael Kent Smith; Deer skull by Marigan O'Malley.

Wikimedia Commons/ Licensed under Public Domain via Wikimedia Commons: (https://commons.wikimedia.org) https://commons.wikimedia.org/wiki/Commons:Simple_media_reuse_guide In accordance with U.S. copyright law: The following original art works were published anywhere before 1928 and therefore are in public domain in the United States. Under the rule in Bridgeman Art Library v. Corel Corporation, a mere 'record' photograph of a 2D work of art (i.e. a photograph which is an as-accurate-as-possible copy of the original) acquires no copyright protection.

The following Wikipedia Commons images are marked *{{PD-US-expired}} unless noted otherwise. {{PD-US-expired}} indicates that a work is in the public domain in the United States because it was published (or registered with the U.S. Copyright Office) before January 1, 1928.

The card illustrations for *The High Priestess, The Sun,* the *Seven of AEther,* and the *Seven of Fungi* incorporate collage elements from source images licensed under the "share alike license" of CC BY-SA 3.0. The collage images have been shared at http://www.boadiceastarot.com under the same license.

Wikimedia Commons:

- By Nicolai Abildgaard (d. 1809), *Jupiter Weighing the Fate of Man,* 1793, Public Domain, https://commons.wikimedia.org/w/index.php?curid=3268342*

- By Andreas Achenbach (d. 1910), *Clearing Up, Coast of Sicily,* 1847, Walters Art Museum, Public Domain, https://commons.wikimedia.org/w/index.php?curid=18782642*

- By Andreas Achenbach (d. 1910), *Surf on a Rocky Coast,* circa 1835, The Bridgeman Art Library, Object 204876, Public Domain, https://commons.wikimedia.org/w/index.php?curid=23834711*

- By Oswald Achenbach (d.1905), *Fireworks in Naples,* 1875 http://www.arthermitage.org/Oswald-Achenbach/Fireworks-in-Naples.html, Public Domain, https://commons.wikimedia.org/w/index.php?curid=22400502*

- By Pieter Aertsen (d.1575), *The Cook,* 1559, Google Arts & Culture, Plaza Balnco, Genoa, Italy ,Public Domain, https://commons.wikimedia.org/w/index.php?curid=23594990*

- By Alfred-Pierre Joseph Agache (d. 1915), *Alegoria da Fortuna,* 1885, http://www.fflch.usp.br/dh/heros/antigosmodernos/renascimento/boccaccio/amorosa/35.html, Public Domain, https://commons.wikimedia.org/w/index.php?curid=4437036*

- By August Ahlborn-Wuselig (d. 1857), *View into the Heyday of Greece,* 1836, Public Domain, https://commons.wikimedia.org/w/index.php?curid=90641668*, CC.0 1.0

APPENDIX

- By Sir Lawrence Alma-Tadema (d.1912), *The Triumph of Titus: The Flavians*, 1885, Walters Art Museum, Public Domain, https://commons.wikimedia.org/w/index.php?curid=18802885*

- By Lady Laura Theresa Alma-Tadema (d.1909) *A Knock at the Door*, 1897, 1000museums.com, Public Domain, https://commons.wikimedia.org/w/index.php?curid=46393879*

- By Friedrich von Amerling (d.1887) *Countess Julie von Woyna*, 1832, https://www.museum-joanneum.at/neue-galerie-graz/ausstellungen/ausstellungen/rundgang-wer-bist-du/raum-01/julie-von-woyna-geb-freiin-von-krieg-hochfelden, Public Domain, https://commons.wikimedia.org/w/index.php?curid=18966444*

- By Thomas Pollock Anshutz (d. 1912), *A Rose*, 1907, Metropolitan Museum of Art, online collection (The Met object ID 20015545), Public Domain, https://commons.wikimedia.org/w/index.php?curid=25235885*

- By Ivan Konstantinovich Aivazovsky (d.1900 Rossiiskaya imperiya), *The Ninth Wave*, 1850, Public Domain, https://commons.wikimedia.org/w/index.php?curid=21854187*

- By Pedro Américo (d.1905), *The Emperor's Speech (Peter II of Brazil in the opening of the General Assembly)*, 1872, Public Domain, https://commons.wikimedia.org/w/index.php?curid=12246333*

- By Albrecht Samuel Anker (d.1910), *Still Life with two glasses of red wine, a bottle of wine, a corkscrew and a plate of biscuits on a tray*, prior to 1910, The Athenaeum, Public Domain, https://commons.wikimedia.org/w/index.php?curid=26634353php?curid=26634353*

- By Harriet Backer (d.1932), *Chez Moi*, 1887, National Museum of Art, Architecture and Design, Public Domain, https://commons.wikimedia.org/w/index.php?curid=12534134*

- By David Bailly (d.1657), *Self-portrait With Vanitas Symbols*, 1651, Own work, Museum De Lakenhal, Public Domain, https://commons.wikimedia.org/w/index.php?curid=6965640*

- By Domenico di Pace Beccafumi (d.1551), *Christi Höllenfahrt*, Detail: Eva, 1530-1535, The Yorck Project (2002) 10.000 Meisterwerke der Malerei (DVD-ROM), distributed by DIRECTMEDIA Publishing GmbH. ISBN: 3936122202., Public Domain, https://commons.wikimedia.org/w/index.php?curid=147779*, CC BY-SA 3.0

- By Christian Berentz (d.1722), *Still life with Grapes*, prior to 1722, cyfrowe.mnw.art.pl, Public Domain, https://commons.wikimedia.org/w/index.php?curid=30428554*

- By Émile Henri Bernard (d.1941), *The Exotic Dancer*, 1915, Christie's, Public Domain, https://commons.wikimedia.org/w/index.php?curid=17885676*

- By Albert Bierstadt (d.1902), *Lake Scene*, prior to 1902, Public Domain, https://commons.wikimedia.org/w/index.php?curid=19917580*

- By Albert Bierstadt (d.1902), *The Rocky Mountains, Lander's Peak*, 1863, The Metropolitan Museum of Art, online, Public Domain, https://commons.wikimedia.org/w/index.php?curid=17880385*

- By Hans Andersen Brendekilde (d.1942), *Farmhouse with Meadow Flowers*, 1909, Public Domain, https://commons.wikimedia.org/w/index.php?curid=28836127 Public Domain, https://commons.wikimedia.org/w/index.php?curid=28836127*

- By William-Adolphe Bouguereau (d.1905), *Zenobia found by Shepherds on the banks of the Araxes*, 1850, praeraffaeliten.de, Public Domain, https://commons.wikimedia.org/w/index.php?curid=1292631*

- By Antonietta Brandeis (d.1926), *Palazzo*, 1910, http://www.dorotheum.com/, Public Domain, https://commons.wikimedia.org/w/index.php?curid=48299700*

- By Antonietta Brandeis (d.1926), *The Rialto Bridge*, 1910, artrenewal.org, Public Domain, https://commons.wikimedia.org/w/index.php?curid=21794817*

- By Antonietta Brandeis (d.1926), *A Venetian Canal*, prior to 1926, Public Domain, https://commons.wikimedia.org/w/index.php?curid=21795921*

- By William Bradford (d. 1892), *Abandoned in the Arctic Ice Fields*, 1876, High Museum of Art, Wmpearl own work, Public Domain, https://commons.wikimedia.org/w/index.php?curid=30673000*

- By William Bradford (d. 1892), *Labrador Fishing Boats near Cape Charles*, 1860, http://www.the-athenaeum.org/art/detail.php?ID=16241, Public Domain, https://commons.wikimedia.org/w/index.php?curid=4488240*

- By Pieter Bruegel the Elder (d.1569), *The Fight Between Carnival and Lent*, 1559, http://insidebruegel.net/, Public Domain, https://commons.wikimedia.org/w/index.php?curid=76436743*

- By Karl Pavlovich Bryullov (d.1852), *The Last Day of Pompeii*, 1830–1833, tAFrCGFUhXM8Jg at Google Cultural Institute, Public Domain, https://commons.wikimedia.org/w/index.php?curid=21863469*

- By Sir Edward Coley Burne-Jones (d.1898), *The Birth of Pegasus and Chrysaor*, circa 1876-1885, http://cgfa.dotsrc.org/burne/p-burne41.htm, Public Domain, https://commons.wikimedia.org/w/index.php?curid=7548412*

- By Alexandre Cabanel (d.1889), *The Birth of Venus*, 1863, Google Art Project, Public Domain, https://commons.wikimedia.org/w/index.php?curid=20264780*

- By Alexandre Cabanel (d.1889), *Samson and Delilah*, 1878, The Athenaeum, Public Domain, https://commons.wikimedia.org/w/index.php?curid=10362434*

- By Canaletto (d.1768), *Alnwick Castle in Northumberland, England*, circa 1752, The Bridgeman Art Library, Object 5574, Public Domain, https://commons.wikimedia.org/w/index.php?curid=17678903*

- By Michelangelo Merisi da Caravaggio (d.1610), *Madonna del Rosario*, 1607, Web Gallery of Art, Public Domain, https://commons.wikimedia.org/w/index.php?curid=15494145*

- By Frederic Edwin Church (d.1900), *Aegean Sea*, circa 1877, Line1983. wordpress.com, Public Domain, https://commons.wikimedia.org/w/index.php?curid=14754482*

- By Frederic Edwin Church (d.1900), *Aurora Borealis*, 1865, 3QGtI0P71obkqA at Google Cultural Institute, Public Domain, https://commons.wikimedia.org/w/index.php?curid=21977254*

- By Frederic Edwin Church (d. 1900), *A Country Home*, 1854, Seattle Art Museum, Public Domain, https://commons.wikimedia.org/w/index.php?curid=16461869*

- By Frederic Edwin Church (d.1900), *Niagara*, 1857, Web Gallery of Art, The Bridgeman Art Library, Object 445386#National Gallery of Art, Washington, D. C., online collection, Public Domain, https://commons.wikimedia.org/w/index.php?curid=15452398*

- By Frederic Edwin Church (d.1900), *Rainy Season in the Tropics*, 1866, FgEWDU2Lt9aDKA at Google Cultural Institute , Public Domain, https://commons.wikimedia.org/w/index.php?curid=22007531*

APPENDIX

- By Frederic Edwin Church (d.1900), *Twilight in the Wilderness*, 1860, http://www.clevelandart.org/art/1965.233, Public Domain, https://commons.wikimedia.org/w/index.php?curid=73554290*
- By George V. Cole (d. 1893), *Hayfield, near Days' Lock, Oxon*, 1891, Public Domain, https://commons.wikimedia.org/w/index.php?curid=23601402*
- By John Collier (d,1934), *Priestess of Delphi*, 1891, Art Gallery of South Australia, Public Domain, https://commons.wikimedia.org/w/index.php?curid=1077695*
- By John Collier (d.1934), *The White Devil*, 1909, Public Domain, https://commons.wikimedia.org/w/index.php?curid=28659330*
- By Colin Campbell Cooper (d.1937), *Taj Mahal, Afternoon*, circa 1913, http://www.heckscher.org/downloads/ED08_EdRes_ExhiGuide_CCC_ProjVers.pdf, Public Domain, https://commons.wikimedia.org/w/index.php?curid=14804951*
- By Gustave Courbet (d.1877), *Portrait of Louis Guéymard in the title role of Giacomo Meyerbeer's opera Robert le diable*, 1857, https://www.metmuseum.org, Public Domain, https://commons.wikimedia.org/w/index.php?curid=8128438*
- By Charles Courtney Curran (d.1942), *Lotus Lilies*, 1888, Public Domain, https://commons.wikimedia.org/w/index.php?curid=23821678*
- By Lucas Cranach the Elder (d.1553), *Portrait of Moritz Büchner*, circa 1520, The AMICA Library2. The Minneapolis Institute of Arts, Public Domain, https://commons.wikimedia.org/w/index.php?curid=18925317*
- By Charles Harold Davis (d. August 1933), *The Brook*, 1890, Wmpearl own work, https://commons.wikimedia.org/w/index.php?curid=18427280*, CCO
- By Paul Delaroche (d. 1856), *The execution of Lady Jane Grey in the Tower of London in the year 1554*, 1833, The National Gallery online, Public Domain, https://commons.wikimedia.org/w/index.php?curid=17589386*
- By Jean-Baptiste Frédéric Desmarais (d.1813) *Le Berger Pâris*, 1787, Public Domain, https://commons.wikimedia.org/w/index.php?curid=29835881*
- By Gerrit Dou (d.1675) *Dentist by Candlelight*, circa 1660-65, Kimbell Art Museum, Public Domain, https://commons.wikimedia.org/w/index.php?curid=7115808*
- By Nikolay Nikanorovich Dubovskoy (d.1918), *Cottage in Sillamägi*, 1907, Public Domain, https://commons.wikimedia.org/w/index.php?curid=10731803*
- By Nikolay Nikanorovich Dubovskoy (d.1918), *Twilight in the Alps*, 1909, Public Domain, https://commons.wikimedia.org/w/index.php?curid=10765367*
- By Asher Brown Durand (d. 1886), *Rocky Cliff*, circa 1860, The Athenaeum, Reynolda House Museum of American Art, Public Domain, https://commons.wikimedia.org/w/index.php?curid=10278566*
- By Albrecht Dürer (d.1528), *Wing of a Roller*, 1512, Web Gallery of Art, Public Domain, https://commons.wikimedia.org/w/index.php?curid=15495178*
- By Friedrich Dürck (d.1884), *Prinz Octavius of Bavaria, King of Greece*, http://www.hdbg.eu/koenigreich/web/index.php/objekte/index/herrscher_id/2/id/953, Public Domain, https://commons.wikimedia.org/w/index.php?curid=17421646*
- By Anthony van Dyck (d.1641), *Lady Shirley*, c.1622, The Yorck Project (2002) 10.000 Meisterwerke der Malerei (DVD-ROM), distributed by DIRECTMEDIA Publishing GmbH. ISBN: 3936122202. https://nttreasurehunt.wordpress.com/2011/11/01/role-reversal/ image, Public Domain, https://commons.wikimedia.org/w/index.php?curid=150537*, CC BY-SA 3.0
- By Anthony van Dyck (d.1641), *Paolina Adorno Brignole-Sale*, 1627, SwHpxHf-WFph0w at Google Cultural Institute, Public Domain, https://commons.wikimedia.org/w/index.php?curid=23594415*
- By Anthony van Dyck (d.1641), *Portrait of a Man in Armor*, 1616/1627, Google Art Project.jpg, 0gFXzQWzQpqB5Q at Google Cultural Institute, Public Domain, https://commons.wikimedia.org/w/index.php?curid=29697396*
- By Josephus Laurentius Dyckmans (d.1888), *A Helping Hand*, 1875, Public Domain, https://commons.wikimedia.org/w/index.php?curid=45207504*
- By Christoffer Wilhelm Eckersberg (d.1853), *The Cloisters of San Lorenzo fuori le mura in Rome*, circa 1815, Own work, Public Domain, https://commons.wikimedia.org/w/index.php?curid=1929059*
- By Christoffer Wilhelm Eckersberg (d.1853), *Standing male model Carl Frørup*, 1837, artsy.net, Public Domain, https://commons.wikimedia.org/w/index.php?curid=48487942*
- By Albert Gustaf Aristides Edelfelt (d.1905), *The Garden at Haikko / Haikon Pu-tarhasta*, 1887, Public Domain, https://commons.wikimedia.org/w/index.php?curid=23542374*
- By Caspar David Friedrich (d.1840), *Northern Sea in the Moonlight*, 1824, National Gallery in Prague, Public Domain, https://commons.wikimedia.org/w/index.php?curid=21996959*
- By Caspar David Friedrich (d.1840), *Owl on a Tree*, prior to 1834, artnet.de2. artinvestment.ru, Public Domain, https://commons.wikimedia.org/w/index.php?curid=17722905*
- By Caspar David Friedrich (d.1840), *Woman at a Window*, 1822. Photo by Sailko - Own work, CC BY 3.0, https://commons.wikimedia.org/w/index.php?curid=88822159*
- By Caspar David Friedrich (d.1840), *Sunset (Brothers) or Evening Landscape with Two Men*, between 1830 and 1835, Web Gallery of Art, Public Domain, https://commons.wikimedia.org/w/index.php?curid=15393898*
- By Orazio Lomi Gentileschi (d.1639), *Danaë*, circa 1623, Getty Research Institute's Open Content Program, Public Domain, https://commons.wikimedia.org/w/index.php?curid=45865888*
- By Baron François Gérard (d.1837), *Joséphine in Coronation Costume*, 1807-1808, Public Domain, https://commons.wikimedia.org/w/index.php?curid=21977121*
- By Jean-Louis André Théodore Géricault (d.1824), *An Officer of the Imperial Horse Guards Charging*, prior to 1824, Public Domain, https://commons.wikimedia.org/w/index.php?curid=7987219*
- By Jean-Léon Gérôme (d.1904), *Bashi-Bazouk*, 1869, Metropolitan Museum of Art, online collection (The Met object ID 440723) Met Open Access policy, Public Domain, https://commons.wikimedia.org/w/index.php?curid=1758280*
- By Jean-Léon Gérôme (d.1904), *Le Barde Noir*, circa 1888, Public Domain, https://commons.wikimedia.org/w/index.php?curid=55028423*
- By Jean-Léon Gérôme (d.1904), *Master of the Hounds*, 1871, Public Domain, https://commons.wikimedia.org/w/index.php?curid=2679816*
- By Pierre Gobert (d.1744), *Portrait of Léopold Clément de Lorraine, Hereditary Prince of Lorraine*, 1710, By anonymous - 3.bp.blogspot.com, Public Domain, https://commons.wikimedia.org/w/index.php?curid=9042893*

APPENDIX

- By John William Godward (d.1922), *The Mirror*, 1899, Art Renewal Center Museum, image 11596, Public Domain, https://commons.wikimedia.org/w/index.php?curid=2354492*

- By Charles Joseph Grips (d.1920), *A Domestic Interior*, 1881, Public Domain, https://commons.wikimedia.org/w/index.php?curid=30651599*

- By Josef Theodor Hansen (d.1912), *Abazia di S.Gregorio, Venice*, 1884, Public Domain, https://commons.wikimedia.org/w/index.php?curid=69905956*

- By Johann Peter Hasenclever (d.1853), *Hieronymus Jobs at His Exam*, 1840, Web Gallery of Art, Public Domain, https://commons.wikimedia.org/w/index.php?curid=15394880*

- By Johann Peter Hasenclever (d.1853), *Die Sentimentale*, circa 1846, Galerie Bassenge, Public Domain, https://commons.wikimedia.org/w/index.php?curid=21006858*

- By Francesco Hayez (d.1882), *Ballerina Carlotta Chabert as Venus*, 1830, enjoymuseum.com, Public Domain, https://commons.wikimedia.org/w/index.php?curid=117796681*

- By Jan Davidsz de Heem (d.1684), *Garland of Flowers and Fruit with the Portrait of Prince William III of Orange*, circa 1670, Web Gallery of Art, Public Domain, https://commons.wikimedia.org/w/index.php?curid=15394935*

- By Carl von der Hellen (d.1902), *Burg Wohldenberg bei Hildesheim*, 1868, Public Domain, https://commons.wikimedia.org/w/index.php?curid=22671303*

- By Jan van der Heyden (d.1712), *Room Corner with Curiosities*, 1712, http://www.wga.hu/html/h/heyden/rarities.html, Public Domain, https://commons.wikimedia.org/w/index.php?curid=7905848*

- By D. Howard Hitchcock (d.1943), *Halemaumau Crater, Kilauea Volcano*, 1889, Lyman House Memorial Museum, Public Domain, https://commons.wikimedia.org/w/index.php?curid=51772655*

- By Winslow Homer (d.1910), *At the Window*, 1872, The Athenaeum, Public Domain, https://commons.wikimedia.org/w/index.php?curid=5744663*

- By Melchior d'Hondecoeter (d.1695), *Das Vogelkonzert*, 1670, http://www.dorotheum.com/fileadmin/user_upload/bilder/Presse/Gallery_of_Highlights/hondecoeter.jpg, Public Domain, https://commons.wikimedia.org/w/index.php?curid=6519382*

- By Michael Conrad Hirt (d.1671), *A Vanitas Still Life with a candle, an inkwell, a quill pen, a skull and books*, circa 1630, http://images.artnet.com/WebServices/picture.aspx?date=20030530&catalog=17040&gallery=110889&lot=00006&filetype=2, Public Domain, https://commons.wikimedia.org/w/index.php?curid=18121073*

- By William Morris Hunt (d.1879), *Niagara Falls*, 1878, The Athenaeum, The Museum of Fine Arts, Boston, Public Domain, https://commons.wikimedia.org/w/index.php?curid=9945145*

- By Jean-Auguste-Dominique Ingres (d.1867), *Academic study of a male torso*, 1801, pl.pinterest.com, Public Domain, https://commons.wikimedia.org/w/index.php?curid=56314750*

- By Jean-Auguste-Dominique Ingres (d.1867), *Marie-Clotilde-Inès Moitessier*, 1856, Olga's Gallery, Public Domain, https://commons.wikimedia.org/w/index.php?curid=38279*

- By James Inskipp (d.1868), *Study of Poppies*, 1832, Google Art Project-NwEUCQmI1m5Q1Q at Google Cultural Institute, Public Domain, https://commons.wikimedia.org/w/index.php?curid=22152884*

- By Joan de Joanes (Juanes) (d.1579), *Ángel custodio*, prior to 1579, Public Domain, https://commons.wikimedia.org/w/index.php?curid=3510580* .

- By Józef Janowski (d.1938), *Landscape with a Rainbow*, 1901, cyfrowe.mnw.art.pl, Public Domain, https://commons.wikimedia.org/w/index.php?curid=45574530*

- By Ludwig Knaus (d.1910), *Mud Pies*, 1873, Walters Art Museum: Public Domain, https://commons.wikimedia.org/w/index.php?curid=18782903*

- By Anna Stainer-Knittel (d.1915), *Alpenblumen*, by 1915, Dorotheum, Public Domain, https://commons.wikimedia.org/w/index.php?curid=26455880*

- By Ludwig Koch (d.1934), *K.u.k. Offiziere zu Pferd*, prior to 1924, This file was derived from: K.u.k. Offiziere zu Pferd.jpg:.K.u.k._Offiziere_zu_Pferd.jpg: Dr.Boboderivative work: Hic et nunc (talk)2012-01-27 08:13 (UTC), Public Domain, https://commons.wikimedia.org/w/index.php?curid=18180307*

- By Alfred Jan Maksymilian Kowalski (d. 1915), *The Wolf*, circa 1895, Düsseldorfer Auktionshaus, Public Domain, https://commons.wikimedia.org/w/index.php?curid=17430274*

- By Peder Severin Krøyer (d.1909), *Summer Evening at Skagen beach. The artist and his wife*, 1899, ywH85ZHPm21PHg at Google Cultural Institute, zoom level maximum, Public Domain, https://commons.wikimedia.org/w/index.php?curid=29859033*

- By Peder Severin Krøyer (d.1909), *Midsummer's Eve Bonfire on Skagen's Beach*, 1906, Google Cultural Institute and Krøyer - internationalt lys, ISBN 978-87-90597-16-0, p. 319, Public Domain, https://commons.wikimedia.org/w/index.php?curid=35246855*

- By Fredrik Marinus Kruseman (d.1882), *Summer Landscape with Harvesting Farmers*, 1850, Art Renewal Center, Public Domain, https://commons.wikimedia.org/w/index.php?curid=3190793*

- By Arkhip Ivanovich Kuindzhi (d.1910), *Rainbow*, 1900–1905, Public Domain, https://commons.wikimedia.org/w/index.php?curid=23618853*

- By Arkhip Ivanovich Kuindzhi (d.1910), *Waves*, circa 1870s, http://kuinje.ru/, Public Domain, https://commons.wikimedia.org/w/index.php?curid=23618838*

- By Étienne De La Hire (Hyre) (attributed to) (d.1643), Art Collection of Prince Władysław Vasa, detail, 1620, kolekcja.zamok krolewski pl, Public Domain, https://commons.wikimedia.org/w/index.php?curid=4417487*

- By Georges De La Tour (d.1652), *The Penitent Magdalene*, 1625-1650, Web Gallery of Art, Public Domain, https://commons.wikimedia.org/w/index.php?curid=15395303*

- By Georges De La Tour (d.1652), *Saint Sebastian Attended by St. Irene*, circa 1649, Web Gallery of Art, Public Domain, https://commons.wikimedia.org/w/index.php?curid=15395306*

- By Jules Joseph Lefebvre (d.1911), *The Feathered Fan*, 1884, Public Domain, https://commons.wikimedia.org/w/index.php?curid=22116652*

- By Edmund Leighton (d.1922), *Lady in a Garden*, prior to 1922, Art Renewal Center Museum, image 14815., Public Domain, https://commons.wikimedia.org/w/index.php?curid=1794099*

- By Sir Frederic Leighton (d.1896), *Clytie*, circa 1890-1892, http://www.the-athenaeum.org/art/full.php?ID=294, Public Domain, https://commons.wikimedia.org/w/index.php?curid=6860933*

APPENDIX

- By Sir Frederic Leighton (d.1896), *Elijah in the Wilderness*, 1878, uQG9WGfbc10kDw at Google Cultural Institute, Public Domain, https://commons.wikimedia.org/w/index.php?curid=21878932*
- By Sir Frederic Leighton (d.1896), *Odalisque*, 1862, Public Domain, https://commons.wikimedia.org/w/index.php?curid=1669535*
- By Peter Lely (d.1680), *Portrait of a young woman and child, as Venus and Cupid*, prior to 1680, Public Domain, https://commons.wikimedia.org/w/index.php?curid=40918198*
- By Adolphe-Alexandre Lesrel (d.1929), *Pan and Venus*, 1865, Public Domain, https://commons.wikimedia.org/w/index.php?curid=26893585*
- By John Frederick Lewis (d.1876), *Lilium Auratum*, 1871, The Yorck Project (2002) 10.000 Meisterwerke der Malerei (DVD-ROM), distributed by DIRECTMEDIA Publishing GmbH. ISBN: 3936122202., Public Domain, https://commons.wikimedia.org/w/index.php?curid=153849*, CC BY-SA 3.0
- By Eduard Friedrich Leybold (d.1879), *Portrait of a young elegant lady, three-quarter length, in a red dress with an embroidered shawl, standing in a landscape*, 1824, Public Domain, https://commons.wikimedia.org/w/index.php?curid=22940251*
- By William Logsdail (d.1944), *Portrait of Alice Crawford in the role of Olivia, Twelfth Night*, 1907, http://41.media.tumblr.com/46722aa760c2f-872dc2572896381edc4/tumblr_minh8xmU7P1qf46efo1_1280.jpg, Public Domain, https://commons.wikimedia.org/w/index.php?curid=37638462*
- By Lucas Luce (d.1661), *Still Life of Pears and Apples on a Pewter Plate, a Bowl of Grapes in a blue and white porcelain bowl, a Roemer, a façon-de-Venise wine glass, a covered blue and white porcelain pitcher and other objects, all on a table*, 1624, Public Domain, https://commons.wikimedia.org/w/index.php?curid=24348931*
- By Hans Makart (d.1884), *The Falconer*, circa 1880, Own work, Photo taken by Cybershot800i in the Neue Pinakothek, Munich., Public Domain, https://commons.wikimedia.org/w/index.php?curid=15622799*
- By John Martin (d.1854), *Destruction of Tyre*, prior to 1854, gF2vHIFIZ-8p2A at Google Cultural Institute, Public Domain, https://commons.wikimedia.org/w/index.php?curid=21880083*
- By John Martin (d.1854), *Joshua Commanding the Sun to Stand Still upon Gideon*, 1816, This file was donated to Wikimedia Commons as part of a project by the National Gallery of Art. Please see the Gallery's Open Access Policy., Public Domain, https://commons.wikimedia.org/w/index.php?curid=81326886*, CC0
- By Jan Matejko (d.1892), *Self-portrait*, 1892, Public Domain, https://commons.wikimedia.org/w/index.php?curid=553796*
- By Attributed to Adolf von Meckel (d.1905), *Landschaft in Sinai*, 1893, (1856-1893) Dorotheum, Public Domain, https://commons.wikimedia.org/w/index.php?curid=22131953*
- By Adolph Friedrich Erdmann von Menzel (d. 1905), *The Iron Rolling Mill (Modern Cyclopes)*, 1875, Wuselig, Public Domain, https://commons.wikimedia.org/w/index.php?curid=90130045*, CC0
- By Jervis McEntee (d.1891), *A Cliff in the Katskills*, circa 1885, Online Collection of Brooklyn Museum; Photo: Brooklyn Museum, 84.81_SL1.jpg, Public Domain, https://commons.wikimedia.org/w/index.php?curid=10189757*
- By Adolph Friedrich Erdmann von Menzel (d. 1905), *Emilie Menzel am Klavier stehend*, 1866, The Yorck Project (2002) 10.000 Meisterwerke der Malerei (DVD-ROM), distributed by DIRECTMEDIA Publishing GmbH.

ISBN: 3936122202., Public Domain, https://commons.wikimedia.org/w/index.php?curid=155566*, CC BY-SA 3.0
- By Adolph Friedrich Erdmann von Menzel (d. 1905), *The Studio Wall*, 1872, Web Gallery of Art, Public Domain, https://commons.wikimedia.org/w/index.php?curid=6714266*
- By Pál Szinyei Merse (d.1920), *Balloon*, 1882, Fine Arts in Hungary, Public Domain, https://commons.wikimedia.org/w/index.php?curid=5460222*
- By John Everett Millais (d.1896), *Farmer's Daughter*, prior to 1896, Public Domain, https://commons.wikimedia.org/w/index.php?curid=8453324*
- By Wendelin Moosbrugger (d.1849), *Gentleman in Blue-Yellow Uniform*, 1798, The Tansey Collection of Miniatures, Public Domain, https://commons.wikimedia.org/w/index.php?curid=6082095*
- By Jan Miense Molenaer, (d.1668) *Allegory of Vanity*, 1633,Web Gallery of Art: Image Info about artwork, Public Domain, https://commons.wikimedia.org/w/index.php?curid=15463444*
- By Edward Moran (d. 1901), *Burning of the Frigate Philadelphia in the Harbor of Tripoli*, 1897, Naval History and Heritage Command: Photo #: KN-10849, Public Domain, https://commons.wikimedia.org/w/index.php?curid=323305*
- By Sebastián Muñoz (d.1690), *Marie Louise of Orléans, Queen of Spain, lying in state in the Royal Alcazar of Madrid*, 1689, PD by age., Public Domain, https://commons.wikimedia.org/w/index.php?curid=8149707*
- By Juan Luna y Novicio (d.1899), *The Roman Maidens*, 1882, Public Domain, https://commons.wikimedia.org/w/index.php?curid=5463723*
- By Joseph Denis Odevaere (d.1830), *Lord Byron on his Death-bed*, c. 1826, Web Gallery of Art: Image ß Info about artwork, Public Domain, https://commons.wikimedia.org/w/index.php?curid=3303327*
- By Balthasar Paul Ommeganck (d.1826), *A Horse*, between 1770 and 1826, http://christchurchartgallery.org.nz/collection/objects/73-260/, Public Domain, https://commons.wikimedia.org/w/index.php?curid=37558473*
- By Parmigianino (d.1540), *Portrait of a Man with a Book*, circa 1524, York Museums Trust Online Collection, Public Domain, https://commons.wikimedia.org/w/index.php?curid=8572787*
- By Antonio de Pereda (d.1678), *Allegory of Vanity*, 1632–1636, 2AEBd_YfJdcAvg at Google Cultural Institute, Public Domain, https://commons.wikimedia.org/w/index.php?curid=21980088*
- By Antonio de Pereda (d.1678), *The Knight's Dream*, circa 1650, Public Domain, https://commons.wikimedia.org/w/index.php?curid=1169885*
- By Léon-Jean-Bazille Perrault (d.1908), *La Tarantella*, prior to 1879, http://novostey.net/leon-jean-basile-perrault/, Public Domain, https://commons.wikimedia.org/w/index.php?curid=37902176*
- By Franz Xaver Andreas Petter (d.1866), *Stillleben mit Weintrauben und Pistole*, 1856, http://www.dorotheum.com/, Public Domain, https://commons.wikimedia.org/w/index.php?curid=48335134*
- By Valentine Cameron Prinsep (d.1904), *The Lady of the Tooti-Nameh or The Legend of the Parrot*, prior to 1904, Public Domain, https://commons.wikimedia.org/w/index.php?curid=15038689*
- By Raphael (d.1520), *Saint George and the Dragon*, circa 1506, hwGXaBhHtRkZIg at Google Cultural Institute, Public Domain, https://commons.wikimedia.org/w/index.php?curid=22173993*

APPENDIX

- By Alexandre-Georges-Henri Regnault (d.1871), *Automedon with the Horses of Achilles*, 1868, Web Gallery of Art, Public Domain, https://commons.wikimedia.org/w/index.php?curid=6385005*
- By Frederic Remington (d.1909), *Moonlight, Wolf*, pre-1909, Addison Gallery of American Art, Public Domain, https://commons.wikimedia.org/w/index.php?curid=24985235*
- By Rembrandt van Rijn (d.1669) (attributed to), *Pallas Athena*, circa 1655, Yelkrokoyade, Public Domain, https://commons.wikimedia.org/w/index.php?curid=40085947*
- By Pierre-Auguste Renoir (d.1919), *Sleeping Cat*, 1862, WikiPaintings, Public Domain, https://commons.wikimedia.org/w/index.php?curid=25175450*
- By William Trost Richards (d.1905), *The Rainbow / Coming Rain, Atlantic City, New Jersey*, 1890, Minnesota Marine Art Museum, Public Domain, https://commons.wikimedia.org/w/index.php?curid=26489331*
- By Hubert Robert (d.1808), *Fire in Rome*, 1787, http://www.arthermitage.org/Hubert-Robert/Fire.jpg, Public Domain, https://commons.wikimedia.org/w/index.php?curid=38251043*
- By David Roberts (d.1864), *The Siege and Destruction of Jerusalem by the Romans Under the Command of Titus, A.D. 70*, 1850, http://jerusalem.nottingham.ac.uk/items/show/62, Public Domain, https://commons.wikimedia.org/w/index.php?curid=3267412*
- By Johan Georg Otto von Rosen (d.1923), *The Explorer (Adolf Erik Nordenskiöld)*, 1886, www.nationalmuseum.se, Public Domain, https://commons.wikimedia.org/w/index.php?curid=518165*
- By Alexander Roslin (d.1793), *Portrait of King Christian VII of Denmark*, 1772, Public Domain, https://commons.wikimedia.org/w/index.php?curid=19389278*
- By Jacob van Ruisdael (d.1682), *View of Haarlem with Bleaching Grounds*, circa 1665, Web Gallery of Art: Image Info about artwork, Public Domain, https://commons.wikimedia.org/w/index.php?curid=6052815*
- By Jan Rustem (d.1835), *Portrait of Maria Mirska, Adam Napoleon Mirski and Barbara Szumska*, circa 1808, National Museum in Warsaw, Public Domain, https://commons.wikimedia.org/w/index.php?curid=98846701*
- By Hubert Sattler (d.1904), *Pyramiden von Gizeh*, prior to 1904, http://www.smca.at/sattler/kosmoramen.html, Public Domain, https://commons.wikimedia.org/w/index.php?curid=10955229*
- By Rubens Santoro (d.1941), *A Venetian Backwater*, circa 1911, http://www.oneoflady.com/2013/07/rubens-santoro.html, Public Domain, https://commons.wikimedia.org/w/index.php?curid=38292353*
- By Godfried Schalcken (d. 1706), *Girl Eating an Apple*, between 1675 and 1680, Web Gallery of Art: Image Info about artwork, Public Domain, https://commons.wikimedia.org/w/index.php?curid=6446486*
- By Ivan Shishkin (d.1898), *Oak Grove*, 1887, Public Domain, https://commons.wikimedia.org/w/index.php?curid=55827808*
- By Frans Snyders (d.1657), *Cook with Food*, 1630s, http://www.wallraf.museum/sammlungen/barock/rundgang/raum-3/, Public Domain, https://commons.wikimedia.org/w/index.php?curid=15397980*
- By Jan Havickszoon Steen (d.1679), *Selbstporträt als Lautenist*, circa late 1600s, The Yorck Project (2002) 10.000 Meisterwerke der Malerei (DVD-ROM), distributed by DIRECTMEDIA Publishing GmbH. ISBN: 3936122202., Public Domain, https://commons.wikimedia.org/w/index.php?curid=159173*, CC BY-SA 3.0

- By Alfred Émile Léopold Stevens (d.1906), *Will you go out with me, Fido?*, http://venetianred.net/2008/12/12/from-mughals-to-minis-the-enduring-paisley-pinecone/, Public Domain, https://commons.wikimedia.org/w/index.php?curid=22856414*
- By George Stubbs, (d.1806), *Hound Coursing a Stag*, circa 1762, lQFnLYKioWmaXg at Google Cultural Institute, Public Domain, https://commons.wikimedia.org/w/index.php?curid=21885996*
- By George Stubbs, (d.1806), *A Monkey*, 1799, xAEBfnkFVM3Tgw at Google Cultural Institute, Public Domain, https://commons.wikimedia.org/w/index.php?curid=21878958*
- By Simon Peter Tilemann (d.1668), *Simon VI. zur Lippe*, after 1663, http://www.llb-detmold.de/sammlungen/literaturarchiv/stammbuecher.html, Public Domain, https://commons.wikimedia.org/w/index.php?curid=10268898*
- By James Tissot (d.1902), *The Poor Lazarus at the Rich Man's Door*, between 1886 and 1894, Online Collection of Brooklyn Museum; Photo: Brooklyn Museum, 2008, 00.159.127_PS2.jpg, Public Domain, https://commons.wikimedia.org/w/index.php?curid=10957406*
- By James Tissot (d.1902), *Young Lady in a Boat*, 1870, Public Domain, https://commons.wikimedia.org/w/index.php?curid=2562484*
- By Gyula Tornai (d.1928), *The Moorish Smoker*, prior to 1928, Art Renewal CenterInfoPic, Public Domain, https://commons.wikimedia.org/w/index.php?curid=19017845*
- By Unknown Master, Dutch (active in the 1620s in Leiden), *Still Life with Books*, 1620s, Web Gallery of Art, Public Domain, https://commons.wikimedia.org/w/index.php?curid=15418050*
- By Viktor Mikhaylovich Vasnetsov (d.1926), *Sirin and Alkonost–Birds of Joy and Sorrow*, 1896, A. K. Lazuko: Victor Vasnetsov. Leningrad: Khudozhnik RSFSR, 1990, ISBN 5-7370-0107-5, Public Domain, https://commons.wikimedia.org/w/index.php?curid=216018*
- By Eugène Joseph Verboeckhoven (d.1881), *Ass and Hens in the Barn*, 1863, Public Domain, https://commons.wikimedia.org/w/index.php?curid=17224078*
- By Vasily Vasilyevich Vereshchagin (d.1904), *A Rich Kyrgyz Hunter with a Falcon*, 1871, http://www.picture.art-catalog.ru/picture.php?id_picture=2401, Public Domain, https://commons.wikimedia.org/w/index.php?curid=3125015*
- By Vasily Vasilyevich Vereshchagin (d.1904), *Людоед (Cannibal)*, 1870-1880, Public Domain, http://www.art-catalog.ru/picture.php?id_picture=2512, https://commons.wikimedia.org/wiki/File:Людоед.jpg#/media/File:Людоед.jpg*
- By Johannes Vermeer (d.1675), *Girl reading a Letter at an Open Window*, circa 1658, 3wFQaidzxA5mqg — Google Arts & Culture, Public Domain, https://commons.wikimedia.org/w/index.php?curid=21963587*
- By Claude-Joseph Vernet (d. 1789), *Seaport by Moonlight*, 1771, Web Gallery of Art: Info about artwork2. gallerix.ru, Public Domain, https://commons.wikimedia.org/w/index.php?curid=6696937*
- By Claude Vignon (d.1670), *Flora*, 1630s, Web Gallery of Art, Public Domain, https://commons.wikimedia.org/w/index.php?curid=15466426*
- By Pauwel de Vos (d.1678) and Jan Wildens (d.1653), *Stag Hunt*, 1630s, Own work, Public Domain, https://commons.wikimedia.org/w/index.php?curid=34157839*

APPENDIX

- By Ferdinand Georg Waldmüller (d.1865), *The Love Letter,* 1849, dorotheum.com, Public Domain, https://commons.wikimedia.org/w/index.php?curid=28936180*
- By Franz Xaver Winterhalter (d.1873), *Eugénie, Empress Consort of the French,* 1864, Transferred from en.wikipedia; transferred to Commons by User: LordT using CommonsHelper, original uploader was Sstjean at en.wikipedia, Public Domain, https://commons.wikimedia.org/w/index.php?curid=4219310*
- By Joseph Wright of Derby (d.1797), *Bridge through a Cavern, Moonlight,* 1907, http://cultured.com, Public Domain, https://commons.wikimedia.org/w/index.php?curid=15588590*
- By Joseph Wright of Derby (d.1797), *Cavern, Near Naples,* 1774, cgH2r_GokULDVw at Google Cultural Institute, Public Domain, https://commons.wikimedia.org/w/index.php?curid=21971185*
- By Joseph Wright of Derby (d.1797), *Vesuvius from Posillipo,* prior to 1797, PAH0TLNJM1xYxg — Google Arts & Culture, Public Domain, https://commons.wikimedia.org/w/index.php?curid=21994784*
- By Albert Žamett (d.1876), *Cascade and Sibyl Temple at Tivoli,* 1855, http://www.art11.ru/zhamet/1b.jpg, Public Domain, https://commons.wikimedia.org/w/index.php?curid=40204464*

Wikimedia Commons–Public Domain Images of Three Dimensional Art:
- By Alexandros of Antioch, *Venus de Milo (Aphrodite from Melos),* ca. 130-100 BC, photographer Jastrow (2007) "I, the copyright holder of this work, release this work into the public domain. This applies worldwide."
- By Anonymous, architectural detail, Marble plaque showing a pomegranate, Granada, Spain, photo by Jebulon, "This file is made available under the Creative Commons CC0 1.0 Universal Public Domain Dedication."
- By Anonymous, Gothic-Style Bracelet, Austrian, circa 1870, Walters Art Museum, Baltimore, MD, "The Walters Art Museum believes that digital images of its collection extend the reach of the museum. To facilitate access and usability, we choose to make digital images of artworks believed to be in the public domain available for use without limitation, rights- and royalty- free., (...) it has adopted the Creative Commons Zero: No Rights Reserved or CC0 license to waive copyright and allow for unrestricted use of digital images and metadata by any person, for any purpose."
- By Anonymous, Ancient Celtic Votive Wheels, photographed at the Musee d'Archeologie Nationale, by PHGCOM (released to public domain by the photographer, (CC0)
- By Anonymous, Stained glass window, early Gothic period, ca.1220, ancient church of Varennes-Jarcy, Île de France. National Museum of the Middle Ages, Paris. Photo by Jebulon,, "This file is made available under the Creative Commons CC0 1.0 Universal Public Domain Dedication." (This is a featured picture on Wikimedia Commons)
- By Workshop of Athens, *Amphora,* photo by Jastrow/Reuse/ Marie-Lan Nguyen, 2006, Marie-Lan Nguyen / released to public domain by the photographer (CC0)

Wikimedia Commons–Commercial Art:
- By Delcampe, *Jeune bedouine tenue de danse,* early 1900s, ES Postcard, Public Domain, https://commons.wikimedia.org/w/index.php?curid=20357012*
- By Karl Richard Lepsius (d.1884), Lepsius-Projekt Sachsen-Anhalt, between 1849 and 1859 (Egyptology illustrations), Public Domain, https://commons.wikimedia.org/w/index.php?curid=2347386*

- By Frères Neurdein, *Postcard of a Young Algerian,* 1920, Delcampe, Public Domain, https://commons.wikimedia.org/w/index.php?curid=20357049*
- Not credited, New Orleans Mardi Gras: printed invitation to the Krewe of Nereus Carnival Ball, 1900, with "Time Flies" motif, Public Domain, https://commons.wikimedia.org/w/index.php?curid=3265694*
- By Frank Reynolds (d.1853), *David and Emily,* 1910, illustration from *The Personal History of David Copperfield,* Toronto Musson Book Co., 1910, Public Domain, https://commons.wikimedia.org/w/index.php?curid=18068476*
- By Unknown, *Profile of a fire boat wrecked on the shore in front of Saint-Malo,* 1692-1693, print, Gallica.fr, Public Domain, https://commons.wikimedia.org/w/index.php?curid=27062442*
- By Unknown author, *Greetings from Krampus,* prior to 1924, greeting card illustration, Historie čertů KrampusUploaded by Kohelet, Public Domain, https://commons.wikimedia.org/w/index.php?curid=27970733*
- By Unknown, *Pointwork at London Bridge Station,* photo from CJ Allen, Steel Highway, 1928, By Andy Dingley (scanner) - Scan from Allen, Cecil J. (1928) *The Steel Highway,* London: Longmans, Green & Co., pp. facing page. 105 (I), Public Domain, https://commons.wikimedia.org/w/index.php?curid=10717363*

Wikimedia Commons–Natural History:
- By John James Audubon (d.1851), *King Duck 1.Male 2.Female,* c.1840, Internet Archive Book Images - https://www.flickr.com/photos/internetarchivebookimages/14565144849/Source book page: https://archive.org/stream/birdsofamericafr06audu/birdsofamericafr06audu#page/n461/mode/1up, No restrictions, https://commons.wikimedia.org/w/index.php?curid=43885190*
- *Chromolithography by Portail after Auguste Faguet, Amanita muscaria,* 1891, *Dictionnaire de botanique par Henri Ernest Baillon and others.* Paris, Hachette, volume 3, Public Domain, https://commons.wikimedia.org/w/index.php?curid=3493461*
- By Jacques Bouquet Barraband, *psittacus erithacus* (African Grey Parrot), *Histoire Naturelle des Perroquets,* 1805, https://www.biodiversitylibrary.org/page/40064486*, CC BY 2.0
- *Eagle- King of Birds and his Kin, Illustration from Falconry, the Sport of Kings* (1920) National Geographic Society, Washington DC, By Internet Archive Book Images - https://www.flickr.com/photos/internetarchivebookimages/14752463965/Source book page: https://archive.org/stream/cu31924022546653/cu31924022546653#page/n86/mode/1up, No restrictions, https://commons.wikimedia.org/w/index.php?curid=43625217*
- Philip Henry Gosse, *A history of the British sea-anemones and corals,* 1860, By Internet Archive Book Images - https://www.flickr.com/photos/internetarchivebookimages/14595135358/Source book page: https://archive.org/stream/historyofbritish00goss/historyofbritish00goss#page/n260/mode/1up, No restrictions, https://commons.wikimedia.org/w/index.php?curid=43964275*
- *ŒUFS* (Eggs), illustration by Adolphe Millot from *Nouveau Larousse Illustré* [1897-1904], Public Domain, https://commons.wikimedia.org/w/index.php?curid=35780158*
- *Attalea Cocos Sabal species* (Palms), 1916, http://bibliodyssey.blogspot.com/2009/07/historia-naturalis-palmarum.html, By Paul K from Sydney, Australia - Attalea - Cocos - Sabal species, https://commons.wikimedia.org/w/index.php?curid=38877959, CC BY 2.0

APPENDIX

- By Baron Georges Cuvier (d.1832), (Spiders), *The Animal kingdom Arranged in Conformity with its Organization*, 1827, Whittaker, London, (University of Illinois Urbana-Champaign), By Internet Archive Book Images - https://www.flickr.com/photos/internetarchivebookimages/18009411240/, No restrictions, https://commons.wikimedia.org/w/index.php?curid=41818179*

- By Holland, W. J. (William Jacob), (d.1932), *The Butterfly book; a Popular Guide to a Knowledge of the Butterflies of North America*, 1914, Garden City, N. Y., Doubleday, Page & Co. (Biodiversity Heritage Library), https://www.flickr.com/photos/internetarchivebookimages/19891698813/Source book page: https://archive.org/stream/butterflybookpop00smholl/#page/n732/mode/1up, No restrictions, https://commons.wikimedia.org/w/index.php?curid=42287321*

- By Hans Hoffmann (d.1591), *A Hedgehog*, before 1584, The Metropolitan Museum of Art, https://www.flickr.com/photos/eoskins/7249630824/, Public Domain, https://commons.wikimedia.org/w/index.php?curid=23131381*

- By Laurens Jacobsz. van der Vinne (d.1742), *Exotic flowers with a snake in the Hortus Botanicus Leiden*, c. 1740- 1742, Museum Boerhaave, Public Domain, https://commons.wikimedia.org/w/index.php?curid=21927298*

- Giuseppe Jatta, Illustration by Comingio Merculiano *Cefalopodi viventi nel Golfo di Napoli (sistematica)*, 1896, Giuseppe Jatta: Stazione zoologica di Napoli, https://www.flickr.com/photos/biodivlibrary/6105705787, Public Domain, https://commons.wikimedia.org/w/index.php?curid=42739281*

- *Natural History of the Animal Kingdom for the Use of Young People*, Kirby, W. F. (William Forsell), (1844-1912), Schubert, Gotthilf Heinrich von, 1780-1860, butterflies, bats, moths, plants, fungi, sea life, amphibians, etc., Society for Promoting Christian Knowledge (Great Britain), https://www.flickr.com/photos/biodivlibrary/5974367575, Public Domain, https://commons.wikimedia.org/w/index.php?curid=43104462*

- By Wermer, Maréchal, Huet, designers; C. de Lasteyrie, lithograph; Etienne Geoffroy Saint-Hilaire, Frédéric Cuvier, authors of the text, *Erinaceus europaeus*, European hedgehog, colored lithograph, *Histoire Naturelle des Mammifères*, T.III by Étienne Geoffroy Saint-Hilaire and Frédéric Cuvier, 1820. Uploaded, stitched and restored by Jebulon - Bibliothèque nationale de France, Public Domain, https://commons.wikimedia.org/w/index.php?curid=25460527*

- Publisher Joseph Meyer (d.1856), *German Birds of Prey*, Volume 13 of the German illustrated encyclopedia Meyers Konversationslexikon, 4th edition (1885-1890) (MKL online at Retro Bibliothek, work 149, 2009, webpage: retrobib-work-149),By Bibliographisches Institut - Meyers Konversationslexikon, Public Domain, https://commons.wikimedia.org/w/index.php?curid=1107101*

- *Mushrooms of America, edible and poisonous*, Ed. by Julius A. Palmer, Jr., 1885, https://www.biodiversitylibrary.org/page/1274937, By Taylor, Thomas, https://www.flickr.com/photos/biodivlibrary/9245551193, Public Domain, https://commons.wikimedia.org/w/index.php?curid=42783920*

- G. Mütrel, *Hummingbirds*, 1892, Wien: F.A. Brockhaus, By G. Mütrel, Leipzig ; Berlin ; Wien : F.A. Brockhaus - Brockhaus' Konversations-Lexikon v. 2, Public Domain, https://commons.wikimedia.org/w/index.php?curid=34062993*

- By Marie Phisalix, illustrator (d.1946), *Fire salamander (Salamandra salamandra)*, 1922, https://www.biodiversitylibrary.org/page/12749179, https://www.flickr.com/photos/biodivlibrary/7461646214, Public Domain, https://commons.wikimedia.org/w/index.php?curid=43134841*, CC BY 2.0

- By Albin Schmalfuß, *Pfifferling (Cantharellus cibarius)*, 1898, Führer für Pilzfreunde: die am haüfigsten vorkommenden essbaren, verdaächtigen und giftigen Pilze, Zwickau: Förster & Borries, von Edmund Michael ; mit 68 Pilzgruppen, nach der Natur von A. Schmalfuss [1] https://dx.doi.org/10.5962/bhl.title.3898, Public Domain, https://commons.wikimedia.org/w/index.php?curid=1229105*

- By Albin Schmalfuß, *Austernseitling (Pleurotus ostreatus)*, 1897, Führer für Pilzfreunde : die am häufigsten vorkommenden essbaren, verdächtigen und giftigen Pilze / von Edmund Michael ; mit 68 Pilzgruppen, nach der Natur von A. Schmalfuss [1] https://dx.doi.org/10.5962/bhl.title.3898, Public Domain, https://commons.wikimedia.org/w/index.php?curid=1281377*

- By Unknown artist, *Islandic Gerfalcon*, 1759, Royal Armoury, Stockholm, Google Cultural Institute, Google Arts & Culture: Home - pic, Public Domain, https://commons.wikimedia.org/w/index.php?curid=21784617*

- By Clarence Moores Weed (d.1947) *Butterflies Worth Knowing*, 1923, Doubleday, https://www.biodiversitylibrary.org/pageimage/9819020, Public Domain, https://commons.wikimedia.org/w/index.php?curid=44660276*

- By Edmund Weiß , *Leonid Meteor Storm, as seen over North America on the night of November 12-13, 1833*, Published 1888, E. Weiß: "Bilderatlas der Sternenwelt", Public Domain, https://commons.wikimedia.org/w/index.php?curid=562733*

Dover Pictura (https://www.iclipart.com) and Dover Publications / (https://www.barnesandnoble.com) Public domain/rights free clip art compilations: purchased individual images and collections

Art Forms in Nature, by Ernst Haeckel
- Moss, fungi, liverworts, cephalopods, nudibranch, jellyfish and anemones

Audubon Prints, by Dover Publications
- Peregrine Falcons (Duck, Hawks), by John James Audubon
- Plate-357-American-Magpie, by John James Audubon
- Plate-056-Common Raven, old male, by John James Audubon
- Plate-057-American Crow, male, by John James Audubon

Great Botanical Plates of Basilius Besler; by Dover Publications
- Flowers
- Insects, edited by Alan Weller
- Insects and spiders

Sea Life, by Dover Publications and Sea Creatures, by Dover Publications
- Invertebrates, cephalopods and crustaceans

Wings, by Dover Publications
- Bats and bugs

Vintage Label and Posters; by Dover Publications
- Bicycle Poster

Animal Illustrations in Full Color, edited by Carol Belanger Grafton
- Box turtle

120 Great Paintings, edited by Carol Belanger Grafton
- Velázquez (d.1660), *Kitchen Scene with Christ in the House of Martha and Mary*, detail of fish, 1618
- Jan van Eyck (d. 1441), *The Arnolfini Portrait*, 1434
- Paul Delaroche (d.1856), *The Execution of Lady Jane Grey in the Tower of London in the Year 1554*, 1833

120 Great Italian Renaissance Paintings, edited by Carol Belanger Grafton

APPENDIX

- Bernat Martorell (d.1492), *Saint George Killing the Dragon*, 1434-1435

124 Great Paintings of Saints
- Jean-Auguste-Dominique Ingres (d.1867), *Joan of Arc at the Coronation of Charles VII*, 1854

120 Great Paintings of Love and Romance, edited by Carol Belanger Grafton
- John Collier (d.1934), *Tannhäuser in the Venusberg*, 1901
- Jean Auguste Dominique Ingres (d.1867), *Jupiter and Thetis*, 1811
- Jean-Auguste-Dominique Ingres (d.1867), *Raphael and the Fornarina*, 1814

120 Great Orientalism Paintings, edited by Carol Belanger Grafton
- Félix Auguste Clément (d.1888), *Women Selling Water and Oranges on the Road to Heliopolis*, 1872
- Alexandre-Georges-Henri Regnault (d.1871), *Execution without Judgment under the Moorish Kings of Granada*, 1870

120 Great Victorian Fantasy Paintings, edited by Jeff A. Menges
- Sir Lawrence Alma-Tadema (d.1912), *The Roses of Heliogabalus*, 1888
- James Draper (d.1920), *The Water Nymph*, 1908
- Sir Frederic Leighton (d.1896), *Perseus and Andromeda*, 1891
- Gustave Moreau (d.1898), *Oedipus and the Sphinx*, 1864

120 Visions of Heaven and Hell,
- John Martin (d.1854), *The Fallen Angels Entering Pandemonium*, 1841

Vintage Printable (http://vintageprintable.com):
- Animal-Bird-Canaries-and-cage-birds-28-Magpie
- Animal-Bird-Ornithologia, Owl 12
- Animal-Cat- Champion Johnnie Fawe II -
- Animal - Deer - Antlers, various photo
- Animal - Non-human primate - Flying lemurs and bats
- Animal-Animal-head-Deer-Reindeer-Animal-head
- Animal-Curiosity-Coral-Italian-2-2
- Animal-Curiosity-Octopus-Die-Cephalopod-1915-orange1
- Animal-Octopus-Squid
- Animal-Curiosity-Octopus-Die-Cephalopod-1915-white
- Animal-Reptile-French-1831-Lizard-2
- Animal-Slimey-Snail-scene
- Animal-Woodland-Hedgehog-Animals-of-the-Levant
- Apparel - Jewelry - Russian enamelwork
- Art-Haeckel-Nudibranchia
- Art-Advertisement-Entertainment-Animal-Tamer-3
- Botanical-Educational-plate-Edible-fungi
- Botanical-Flora-Batavia-Agaricus-albus-Fries-1410
- Botanical-Flora-Batavia-Agricus-gracilentus-krombh-1370
- Botanical-Flower-Pitcher-Plant-Haeckel
- Botanical-Fungi-On-substrate
- Botanical-Mushroom-Anatomical-color1
- Botanical-Mushroom-Cantharellus-floccosus-Schw.
- Botanical-Mushroom-Edible-and-Poisonous-Mushrooms-Common- Mushroom
- Botanical-Mushroom-Edible-and-Poisonous-Mushrooms-Edible-Blue-Cap
- Botanical-Mushroom-Edible-and-Poisonous-Mushrooms-Edible-Chanterelle-Horn-of-Plenty
- Botanical-Mushroom-With-some-dirt
- Botanical-Bryologica-atlantica-1910-Mosses-lichens-and-liverwarts-5
- Botanical-Bryologica-atlantica-1910-Mosses-lichens-and-liverwarts-12
- Champignon-de-France-LAuriculaire-Tremelloide
- Color-Multi-Botanical-132
- Design-Apparel-Asian-81
- Design-Apparel-Glove-with-flowered-cuff
- Juvenile-Illustration-Wizard-of-Oz-and-Good-Witch1
- Landscape-Painting - Irish 9
- Marbled paper design
- Portrait-Painting-Woman in a yellow dress
- Portrait-Face-Painting-Portrait-of-a-Young-Woman
- Portrait-Illustration-Sleep-3
- Science-Astronomy-Map- Celestial map of constellations visible from France 19th Century

The Public Domain Revue (https://publicdomainreview.org):
- *The Model Book of Calligraphy*, 1561–1596, by Georg Bocskay and Joris Hoefnagel
- *Ernst Haeckel's Bats*, 1904, by Ernst Haeckel
- *America, a Personification*, ca. 1590, engraved by Flemish designer and engraver Adriaen Collaert after a design by Marten de Vos
- *The Temple of Flora*, 1807, by Robert John Thornton
- Moon Model, Field Columbian Museum, 1900, model prepared by Johann Friedrich Julius Schmidt, Germany, in 1898

The Graphics Fairy Vintage Advertising Clip Art (http://thegraphicsfairy.com):
- Butterflies, bees, birdcage, birds, dove, ribbons, owl, strawberries, teacup, spider webs, jackdaw, fly, phrenology illustration, octopus, flowers, foliage

https://freevintageillustrations.com
- Flowers, insects, cephalopods, animals, fungi, spiderweb, dishware

Library of Congress Prints and Photographs Division Washington, D.C. USA (http://hdl.loc.gov/loc.pnp/pp.print):
- Anonymous, *Pearl of the Orient*, Tobacco label, between 1860 and 1870, Major & Knapp Engraving, Manufacturing & Lithographic Co., New York
- *he grand lay-out. Circus parade around tents, with crowd watching alongside railroad train*. Chromolithograph by Gibson & Co., Cincinnati, Ohio, 1874, This image is available from the United States Library of Congress's Prints and Photographs division under the digital ID pga.01329.
- *Tree*, Harris & Ewing, photographer, 1931, Reproduction Number: LC-DIG-hec-36276, Call Number: LC-H2- B-4507 [P&P].
- Wells & Hope Co. (poster publisher) *Belle of Nelson* poster for their sour mash whiskey,1878, Library of Congress, LC-DIG-pga-03041

US Government NASA images (http://www.nasa.gov/multimedia/imagegallery/index.html):
- *Star Forming Region LH 95*, Astronomy Picture of the Day, March 21, 2008, Credit: Hubble Heritage Team, D. Gouliermis (MPI Heidelberg) et

Boadicea's Tarot of Earthly Delights

APPENDIX

al., (STScI/AURA), ESA, NASA, (http://apod.nasa.gov/apod/ap080312.html), {{PD-USGov-NASA}}

- *N44C nebula in the large Magellanic cloud*, Image ID: PIA04225, Image credit: NASA and the Hubble Heritage Team (STScI/AURA) Acknowledgment: D. Garnett (University of Arizona), http://heritage.stsci.edu/2002/12/index.htm, {{PD-USGov-NASA}}l

- *A composite image of the Western hemisphere of the Earth*, 2000, NASA/ GSFC/ NOAA/ USGShttp://antwrp.gsfc.nasa.gov/apod/image/0304/bluemarble2k_big.jpg, {{PD-USGov-NASA}}

- *Jovian Cloud Tops*, 2017, Credit: NASA/JPL-Caltech/SwRI/MSSS/ Bjorn Jonsson,https://photojournal.jpl.nasa.gov/catalog/PIA21391, {{PD-USGov-NASA}}

- Apollo 11 Mission image - *View of moon with Earth on the horizon*, July, 1969, Johnson Space Center, https://images.nasa.gov/details-as11-44-6551.html, {{PD-USGov-NASA}}

- *Earth's Moon, 8 December 2009*, the Galileo spacecraft returned a number of images of Earth's only natural satellite. Galileo surveyed the moon on Dec. 7, 1992, on its way to explore the Jupiter system.NASA/ JPL/USGS, {{PD-USGov-NASA}

US Government NOAA images –Publications of the U.S. Department of Commerce, National Oceanic & Atmospheric Administration (NOAA), NOAA Central Library (http://www.photolib.noaa.gov):

- A reef scene in the Caribbean, reef 1049, NOAA's Coral Kingdom Collection, St. Lucia, Caribbean Sea, August 1988, Photographer: Dr. Anthony R. Picciolo, NOAA NODC, {{PD-USGov-NOAA}}

- Reef scene, reef1448 Pohnpei, Photographer: David Burdick, {{PD-USGov-NOAA}}

- Reef 1025, NOAA's Coral Kingdom Collection, Caribbean Sea, June 1990, Photographer: Dr. Anthony R. Picciolo, NOAA NODC, {{PD-USGov-NOAA}}

- Reef 1249, Round coral w/ purple in foreground,Reef Scene,Mariana Islands, Guam, Photographer: David Burdick, {{PD-USGov-NOAA}}

- Reef 2091, NOAA's Coral Kingdom Collection, Gulf of Aqaba, {{PD-USGov-NOAA}}

- wea00619, NOAA's National Weather Service (NWS) Collection, Lightning Near Boulder Colorado, 1982, Photographer: Commander John Bortniak, NOAA Corps (ret.), {{PD-USGov-NOAA}}

- nssl0012, NOAA's National Severe Storms Laboratory (NSSL) Collection NOAA Photo Library, NOAA Central Library; OAR/ERL/National Severe Storms Laboratory (NSSL), {{PD-USGov-NOAA}}

- nur04502, Voyage To Inner Space - Exploring the Seas With NOAA Collection, Pacific Ocean, Endeavour Ridge, OAR/National Undersea Research Program (NURP), {{PD-USGov-NOAA}}

- nssl0064, The first tornado captured by the NSSL doppler radar and NSSL chase personnel. The tornado is here in its early stage of formation. NOAA's National Severe Storms Laboratory (NSSL) Collection, Union City, Oklahoma, May 24, 1973, NOAA Photo Library, NOAA Central Library; OAR/ERL/National Severe Storms Laboratory (NSSL), {{PD-USGov-NOAA}}

- nssl0112, Mammatus clouds. June, 1973, NOAA Photo Library, NOAA Central Library; OAR/ERL/National Severe Storms Laboratory (NSSL), {{PD-USGov-NOAA}}

- wea00016, NOAA's National Weather Service (NWS) Collection, An aircraft view of high cirrus and stratocumulus undercast with altostratus, Weather Wonders/Clouds/Stratocumulus/Altostratus /Cirrus, {{PD-USGov-NOAA}}

- wea00115, Above the stratocumulus looking at multi-layers of clouds. April 1974, {{PD-USGov-NOAA}}

- wea04754, Lightning, NOAA's National Weather Service (NWS) Collection (license: https://creativecommons.org/licenses/by/2.0) {{PD-USGov-NOAA}}

- amer0303, The northern lights dance over a frozen Lake Superior as the lights of Marquette blaze in the distance. Image ID: amer0303, NOAA's Small World Collection, Marquette, Michigan, Photographer: Mark Stacey, Electronic Technician WSFO Marquette (license: https://creativecommons.org/licenses/by/2.0), {{PD-USGov-NOAA}}

Stock imagery rights managed purchases

iStock (enhanced licenses purchased):

- The 1902 Boudica Statue on Westminster Bridge, London, Credit: davidf / iStock, Stock photo ID:171586410, Upload date: November 03, 2012

- Common Raven (Corvus corax), Credit: Piotr Krzeslak / iStock, Stock photo ID:655197768, Upload date: March 19, 2017

Shutterstock (enhanced licenses purchased):

- Stock Photo ID: 560270, Modern reconstruction of thatched dwelling of Iceni tribe from East Anglia region of Britain, Photo Contributor: Guy Erwood / Shutterstock

- Stock Photo ID: 360964361, Birds- Common Raven (Corvus corax), Photo Contributor: Marcin Perkowski / Shutterstock

- Stock Photo ID: 1542643865, Isolated carrion crow in flight with fully open wings, Photo Contributor: retofuerst / Shutterstock

- Stock Photo ID: 1809618631, Horse chestnut leaves, Photo Contributor: Yurii Romanchuk / Shutterstock

Boadicea's Tarot of Earthly Delights

Paula Millet is a deck creator, collage artist, and graphic designer: I dreamed of creating a Tarot deck inspired by my lifetime of visiting and working for art and science museums—a Tarot that captured the eclectic spirit of these experiences. When I look at art, I see stories unfold. This Tarot's narrative illustrations present readers the opportunity to imagine and interpret their personal tales. I appreciate Tarot primarily for its creative, artistic presentation of rich and complex symbolism and as a portal for self enlightenment.

◇ ◈ ◇

Caroline Kenner is a Witch, a Tarotiste, a priestess, and a healer. She has read Tarot cards for five decades. Caroline is a co-founder and current co-owner of The Fool's Dog Tarot app company. She spent 30 years as a Pagan organizer in the DC area. Caroline is a third-degree Witch, initiated by Janet Farrar and Gavin Bone. Her first Witchcraft teacher was Andras Corban Arthen, in 1984. Caroline's most prominent teachers are Sandra Ingerman, Dolores Ashcroft-Nowicki, and Ivo Dominguez, Jr. Caroline belongs to the Assembly of the Sacred Wheel, building the New Alexandrian Library in Delaware. When she was 16, Caroline worked as an archeological volunteer in Colchester, England, digging down through the black layer of the burned Roman city. Caroline has venerated Boadicea as a Sacred Ancestress for more than fifty years.